PET DEATH

Sandra Helene Straub

Death, Value and Meaning Series
Series Editor: John D. Morgan

LONDON AND NEW YORK

First published 2004 by Baywood Publishing Company, Inc.

Published 2018 by Routledge
2 Park Square, Milton Park, Abingdon, Oxon OX14 4RN
52 Vanderbilt Avenue, New York, NY 10017

Routledge is an imprint of the Taylor & Francis Group, an informa business

Copyright © 2004 Taylor & Francis

All rights reserved. No part of this book may be reprinted or reproduced or utilised in any form or by any electronic, mechanical, or other means, now known or hereafter invented, including photocopying and recording, or in any information storage or retrieval system, without permission in writing from the publishers.

Notice:
Product or corporate names may be trademarks or registered trademarks, and are used only for identification and explanation without intent to infringe.

Library of Congress Catalog Number: 2003058312

Library of Congress Cataloging-in-Publication Data

Straub, Sandra Helene, 1950-
  Pet death / Sandra Helene Straub.
    p. cm. -- (Death, value, and meaning series)
  Includes bibliographical references (p.   ) and index.
  ISBN 0-89503-282-1 (cloth)
  1. Pet owners--Psychology. 2. Pets--Death--Psychological aspects. 3. Bereavement--Psychological aspects. I. Title. II. Series.

SF411.47.S78 2003
155.9'37--dc22

2003058312

ISBN 13: 978-0-89503-282-9 (pbk)
ISBN 13: 978-0-415-78510-5 (hbk)

Dedication

Pet Death is dedicated to all the pets that I have been privileged to share my life with! I am so thankful for the unconditional love they have given and for all the times they comforted me when things weren't right.

I hope to see them all again one day when I cross over the Rainbow Bridge.

    Barney   B. J. (Barney Junior)   Bogey   Bootsy

    Cheskis   Lucy   Mama   Misti   Niggy

Oscar   Pretzel   Sparky   Sunshine   Taffy   Yankee

Hope is the thing with feathers that perches in the soul and sings the tune without the words and never stops . . . at all.
—*Emily Dickinson*

Contents

Foreword vii

Rainbow Bridge ix

Acknowledgment xi

Introduction 1

CHAPTER 1
The Bond between Human and Pet 5

CHAPTER 2
When a Pet Dies Suddenly 9

CHAPTER 3
When a Pet is Euthanized 17

CHAPTER 4
Telling the Children. 33

CHAPTER 5
When the Pet is a Companion 37

CHAPTER 6
The Grief Process 43

CHAPTER 7
Coping with the Loss of Your Pet. 53

CHAPTER 8
Helping the Bereaved Pet Owner. 59

CHAPTER 9
Dealing with Guilt. 63

CHAPTER 10
Do Pets Grieve?. 65

CHAPTER 11
Final Farewells 69

CHAPTER 12
Pets and Spirituality 73

CHAPTER 13
Getting Another Pet. 79

CHAPTER 14
Animal Abuse 83

CHAPTER 15
Healing Activities 97

CHAPTER 16
Happy Endings 109

Glossary 121

Sources of Support 127

Magazines, Journals, and Newsletters. 137

Pet Memorabilia 139

Bibliography 143

Epilogue 151

Index 155

Foreword

I still remember my first pet. He was a black cat we called Jay Jay. He was an independent spirit (like most cats), but as loyal as any dog. He would spend his days exploring the woods near our home, returning each afternoon to greet me as I arrived home from school. Most days he would bring with him the "fresh catch" of the day, which was usually a small fish he snatched from the stream running through our neighborhood. As a child, I loved that cat. Jay Jay was one of my best friends. When I was alone with him I would talk to him about everything. I would tell him my frustrations, my fears, and would pretend he could talk back to me. He brought me comfort when I was sad and companionship when I was lonely.

One day my dad found Jay Jay dead in his favorite bush in front of our house. It appeared as though he had died of natural causes. My father buried him in the far corner of our backyard. He made a marker out of a brick with the inscription, "Jay Jay the Cat, 1978-1980." I remember the intense feelings of sadness I felt as my father told us what had happened. I was so grateful that he had treated Jay Jay with such respect and had marked his grave and recognized the significance of his life. My relationship with Jay Jay the cat continued for a few more years. From time to time I would sit by his marker and tell him my troubles. Spending these times would remind me of the impact he had on me, the amount of comfort he had brought to my life.

Now, when I think back on this experience, I still love that cat. This confirms in my mind what a powerful bond we develop with our pets. In the past few years I have facilitated hundreds of support group sessions with those grieving the death of a loved one. It never fails that someone during the process always shares something about his or her pet(s). At the mention of the topic almost everyone in the room "lights up" and we take turns sharing stories of how our pets have brought us comfort and unconditional love. Many recount the grief and loss they felt after a beloved pet died. The stories are countless.

There was one lady who brought her dog to the support group meeting. This dog would snuggle quietly on her lap throughout the session. The bond between the two was undeniable. She expressed to the group that her dog had brought her great comfort during her husband's illness and companionship now that her husband had died. She did not like to leave him alone at home when he could be with her. So, this little dog became a regular member of our group and we all grew accustomed to his presence.

In this book, Dr. Straub has addressed a topic untouched by many death and dying authors and educators. She has presented a comprehensive guide to the subject of pet loss. If you are grieving the death of a pet, may you find inspiration in these written words as you seek to heal the pain of your loss. If you are a professional grief counselor or a loving friend to someone dealing with grief due to a pet's death, may you gain a greater understanding and appreciation for the bond we humans have with the animal world, finding a new perspective into the grief felt by those who have experienced the death of a pet.

Our pets become significant members of our families. They are our adopted children, our brothers and sisters. The other day my youngest daughter announced with pride, "We have four people in our family!" My oldest child quickly corrected her saying, "No, we have six. You can't forget Zoe (big, fluffy Golden Retriever) and Kitty (big, fat lazy cat)!"

Andy McNiel serves Hospice of Martin & St. Lucie as the Director of Development. He previously served as the Director of Grief Support Services for the Hospice of Martin and St. Lucie, Inc. Mr. McNiel began his work in grief support as a Bereavement Specialist for The Amelia Center, a comprehensive Grief Support Center in Birmingham, Alabama. Mr. McNiel is an experienced public speaker and has offered many presentations on various topics including Stress Management, Understanding the Grieving Process, Healing through Grief, Finding Inspiration during Difficult Times, Children and Grief, Volunteer Leadership, to name a few. Mr. McNiel is also an ordained minister and has served as Minister to Youth at First Baptist Church, Pinson, Alabama and First Baptist Church of Royal Palm Beach, Florida. Mr. McNiel holds a Bachelor of Arts in Religion from Palm Beach Atlantic College and Master of Arts in Counseling from The University of Alabama at Birmingham. He is married and has two daughters (ages 7 and 4).

Rainbow Bridge

Just this side of heaven is a place called Rainbow Bridge. When an animal dies that has been especially close to someone here, that pet goes to Rainbow Bridge. There are meadows and hills for all of our special friends so they can run and play together. There is plenty of food and water and sunshine, and our friends are warm and comfortable. All of the animals who had been ill and old are restored to health and vigor; those who were hurt or maimed are made whole and strong again, just as we remember them in our dreams of days and times gone by.

The animals are happy and content, except for one small thing—they miss someone very special to them who had to be left behind. They all run and play together, but the day comes when one suddenly stops and looks into the distance. The bright eyes are intent; the eager body quivers. Suddenly, one begins to break away from the group, flying over the green grass, legs running faster and faster. YOU have been spotted, and when you and your special friend finally meet, you cling together in joyous reunion, never to be parted again. The happy kisses rain upon your face; your hands again caress the beloved head, and you look once more into the trusting eyes of your pet, so long gone from your life but never absent from your heart.

Then you cross Rainbow Bridge together.

—Author Unknown

Acknowledgments

First of all, I want to thank my editor, John D. Morgan, for his incredible insight and belief in me AGAIN!

As always, Bobbi Olszewski, Production Manager for Baywood Publishing, Inc., has been wonderful in guiding me through book number 3. Thank you for always being available when I need you and for your valued friendship.

I owe a great debt of gratitude to Stu Cohen and his fine staff at Baywood for their continuous support.

Many thanks go out to my students and clients who submitted their pet stories for this book. Even though in many cases it was therapeutic for them to write about their beloved pet, it was still difficult and brought many tears to the surface. They have allowed me to step into their hearts and private journeys.

I thank my friends who accepted me in my sorrow and continue to believe in me.

And last, but certainly not least, I thank my husband, Paul, for being the wind beneath my wings.

> I think dogs are the most amazing creatures; they give unconditional love. For me, they are the role model for being alive.
> —*Gilda Radner (1946–1989)*
> *U.S. actress, comedienne,*
> *"It's Always Something," 1989*

Introduction

If you are anticipating or coping with the significant loss of a pet in your life and wish to better understand the grief that accompanies such a loss, *Pet Death* will provide you with the information, comfort, and support you need. As you travel along your journey of grief, what you'll find on these pages is meant to acknowledge and honor your grief—to help you make some sense out of what you may be feeling. Through these pages, I hope to prepare you for what to expect in grief and to help you find meaning, growth, and healing along the way.

I have found my own way through grief many, many times. As one who has always wanted and needed pets, especially cats, in my life, over the years I have mourned deeply after each loss. In writing *Pet Death*, I have recounted on my own personal experiences and education in mental health counseling to help others understand what they are feeling. The death of a beloved pet is traumatic. Only those who have suffered such a loss can truly know the heartache and pain it produces. Over the years many poets and authors have tried to put into words the feelings in our hearts when we are forced to say goodbye to a pet.

The Power of the Dog

There is sorrow enough in the natural way from men and women to fill our day;
And when we are certain of sorrow in store, why do we always arrange for more?
Brothers and sisters, I bid you beware of giving your heart to a dog to tear.
Buy a pup and your money will buy love unflinching that cannot lie—

> Perfect passion and worship fed by a kick in the ribs or a pat on the head.
> Nevertheless it is hardly fair to risk your heart to a dog to tear.
> When the fourteen years which Nature permits are closing in asthma, or tumour, or fits,
> And the vet's unspoken prescription runs to lethal chambers or loaded guns,
> Then you will find—it's your own affair—but . . . you've given your heart to a dog to tear.
> When the body that lived at your single will,
> With its whimper of welcome, is stilled (how still!).
> When the spirit that answered your every mood is gone—wherever it goes—for good,
> You will discover how much you care, and will give your heart to a dog to tear.
> We've sorrow enough in the natural way, when it comes to burying Christian clay.
> Our loves are not given, but only lent, at compound interest of cent per cent.
> Though it is not always the case, I believe,
> That the longer we've kept 'em, the more do we grieve:
> For, when debts are payable, right or wrong, a short-term loan is as bad as a long—
> So why in—Heaven (before we are there) should we give our hearts to a dog to tear?
>   —*Rudyard Kipling*

The emotional reaction to the death of a pet is determined by our degree of involvement with that animal. The mourning for a pet can be far more intense than for a human. The pain you are experiencing now is very real, and even crippling emotionally. You are actually mourning the death of a very close member of your immediate family. In many ways, the pet becomes an extension of our own personality. Who has not experienced that special sense of awareness and greeting when we put the key in the lock and open the door? Coming home is a major event—no matter how long we were away. We had become so used to anticipating our pet's welcome when we arrived, but now it is insanely silent.

Pet Death was written especially to support those people whose companion animals have died and to allow them to feel whatever is natural for them. Sadly, many who are grieving the death of a pet have their pain increased by the awkwardness or apathy of friends and family. We feel there are not enough people who can comprehend our grief and we must therefore learn to readjust our relationships with others as a defensive behavior. Death, in general, is a subject that most people are very uncomfortable talking about. Discussion of the topic is awkward or even impossible and not well supported in our society. People don't know how to talk about it without embarrassment or evasion. Euphemisms generally attempt to substitute misleading expressions for more specific terms and ideas. You may discover that the death of your beloved pet is too difficult or distressing for some people to comprehend or even be tolerant of. Too often those we rely on most let us down during this very sad time. We are fortunate when we find other pet owners who can share our feelings and responses.

If you are the kind of person who grieves deeply for the loss of a beloved pet, this book is meant for you to read. The information presented in these pages will help you realize that you are not alone. Many others have suffered the same anguish from the death of a cherished animal. *Pet Death* will also teach you about this exceptionally painful and puzzling impact on your life. The shock of bereavement is one of the most profound emotional traumas we can experience. When a pet dies, that special, warm place in our hearts suddenly becomes empty and, as in all painful events, it will take time to get over the loss. But, as time passes, we realize that animals have a way of teaching us about unconditional love, about loyalty, joy, and friendship. And whatever we have shared in their presence can never really be lost.

Many of the things I have written about in this book I learned firsthand during my own heart's journey through the strange land of grief. Through my own pain and needs, and those of my clients, writing *Pet Death* became a necessity. I believe that anyone who loves greatly in life and grieves deeply in loss is deserving of whatever respect, comfort, and support I can offer. I wish you all of these things as you read the pages of this book.

> The love for all living creatures is the noblest attribute of man.
> —*Charles Darwin*

CHAPTER 1

The Bond between Human and Pet

> Everything that lives, lives not alone nor for itself.
> —*William Blake*

The bond between human and pet is one that goes far back into prehistoric times. Cave drawings depict dogs joining in the hunt, as well as sharing life space with our early ancestors. That primitive bonding was a natural interaction, serving the basic needs of both humans and animals. It included mutual protection and companionship along with herding and hunting.

After thousands of years, we now keep companion animals of all kinds for the pure pleasure of their company. They enrich our lives in many different ways and can serve as a playful pal or best friend. There is a basic need for humans to give love and nurture. It begins with children caring for their dolls and toy animals. When we grow up, this loving human instinct is usually transferred to more traditional objects of affection—our pets.

Elderly pet owners tend to be extremely affectionate, even doting on an animal. A pet shares the senior's loneliness and the changes taking place in his or her ability to do things. Whatever losses the older person may have suffered during a lifetime become shared experiences. Pets become whatever we want them to be in our lives and never seem to fail us. We judge ourselves by them. Their companionship gives us added stability and purpose, and a sense of personal enrichment. A person's health and mobility may have deteriorated, but pets love and depend on their owners as much as before. As hearing and sight diminish, so may one's motivation to enjoy life. There are fewer visitors and activities, if any, but that's all right if the senior citizen has the security of a pet as a loving companion. The pet shares everything, and becomes a very dear and necessary part of the senior's life. When the pet shows signs of aging or health deterioration, one's dependency is increased. The pet owner must become even more of a provider and caretaker. The positive side of this is it makes the senior feel even more vital and needed. The mutual interchange of need and caregiving becomes very enriching. When the pet dies, the shock feels like abandonment. It seems as if nobody really cares. Sadly, this often leads to depression in the older person unless there are loving family members and/or friends in their lives. The positive side of this event is the wisdom that comes with experience over the years. The elderly person has seen friends and family members die, and have learned to become more understanding than when at a younger age.

The bond we develop with pets is wonderful and rewarding. It is an active reaching out and sharing of life with another living being that happens not to be human. It offers us a chance to share and express our true selves, without needing to defend our actions or feelings. This extraordinary relationship is founded on unconditional love—feeling accepted and loved regardless of behavior. Pets give us our greatest opportunities to express love without ever having to worry about being judged or rejected. They give us back a devotion that is unmatched by any other relationships. Their obedience and respect give us an increased sense of self-worth and add meaning to our lives. And, in return, they are cherished beyond words. It is this high personal value of pets that can make us more vulnerable in our bereavement when our pets die. The death of a pet confirms that it is the relationship that is most important, not the intrinsic value of its animal object (Lagoni, Butler, & Hetts, 1994). As wonderful as human relationships can be, this relationship often goes far beyond the relationships we have with people. We open up completely to our pets and receive an inner sense of joy and strength at being so loved in return. It has often been said that pets can be truer friends than people. This is because they are never critical, and therefore allow us to blossom emotionally in ways that would not be possible or appropriate with human beings.

The Captain of the Lady Anne

The Captain of the Lady Anne
Was not a sailing man.
Instead he was the kindest soul
That walked upon the land.
He was her faithful guardian

And gave his life he would,
To see his Lady happy
He'd do everything he could.
But one dark night it happened
And his life was quickly gone.
She cried, she hugged and held him
As she sent him on.
While fate does often take away
His time with her not long,
I do believe he still stands watch
Their bond still true and strong.
Sometimes I think she hears him
And feels him brush her hand,
But still there is a sadness
That her heart can hardly stand.
I know that she will see him
In that land so far away,
With her Captain of the Lady Anne
She will run and laugh and play.
—*Patricia McGregor, personal communication*

If we measure lives not in time but in grace, in the joy with which they are lived, and in the love they leave behind, then we have much to learn from our cats.
—*Author Unknown*

CHAPTER 2

When a Pet Dies Suddenly

> There is no greater sorrow than to recall a time of happiness in misery.
>
> —*Dante*

When a pet dies suddenly or unexpectedly or in an accident, this is very traumatic for the owner and feelings of grief are compounded by feelings of anger and often guilt. When there was no time to say good-bye, we are particularly upset. We even feel cheated by not having had the chance to see the pet die naturally. But that isn't easy either. No time is a good time for we are never ready for the death of a pet. There is always the question of "How much control do we have over our fates?" Some philosophers claim that everything that happens is natural and happens for a reason. Even carelessness should be seen in this light. Leaving the puppy outside on a frayed leash or the cat around a plant with poisonous plant leaves are not uncommon happenings. There are other cases, too, like the dog that ran out of the house and was hit by a car, the dog that was seized by an alligator while the owner was fishing, or the sweet little kitten that was carried off by a hawk in front of the horrified owner. What about the man who backed out of his driveway and accidentally ran over his daughter's cat? Following an accident of any kind it is all too easy to say, "If only I had done this instead," but you had no way of knowing that your pet would die. Try to think of the good times you enjoyed together and, although it is difficult, try not to feel guilty about an event you could not have foreseen. Allow yourself to have these feelings of guilt, but remember that you must not blame yourself. Owners are not expected to be psychic and however hard you try to ensure your pet is safe, accidents do indeed happen.

Equally shocking to the owner is the sudden death due to a stroke or heart failure or to an illness or condition where there were no symptoms for you or your veterinarian to detect. Sometimes, unknown to the owner, a pet has been in an accident which left no outward marks, but which caused internal damage. An autopsy, should you request it, may identify the cause of death, but pets very occasionally die for no known reason. It is more upsetting if the pet is young and apparently healthy, but it is very possible that he had a birth defect (such as an abnormal heart) which led to his sudden and unexpected death. You may wish to discuss the death with the veterinary staff. They may not be able to tell you the cause of death, but they can often reassure you that you could not have anticipated or prevented such a sudden death. Again, it is unfair to blame yourself for not noticing warning signs of illness if there was no indication for you to detect.

You will need to decide how to deal with the body if your pet has died in a road traffic accident. If you find the sight of a body too distressing, a friend or neighbor may be able to help you or you could place a towel over it before moving it. If you cannot bury your pet, many veterinarians will allow you to leave his body at the clinic where the body can be dealt with by the veterinarian or be collected by a pet cemetery or pet crematorium if you make appropriate arrangements.

Sadly, a number of pets suddenly disappear and never return. This is very upsetting because you do not know exactly what has happened to your pet and also because there is no body to grieve for. Establishing closure is more difficult for those who are unable to actively see a body. There is always that faint hope that your pet will turn up safe and well one day. This has been a recent experience for me while writing this book. Our cat, Oscar, went outside one day and never returned home. My husband and I searched everywhere for him. We reported the loss to the local animal control agency, humane society, and animal hospitals in the area. I would imagine him waiting to come inside but when I opened the door, Oscar wasn't there. It has been over three months now and still no sign of him. The only hope I have is that he has a new home with someone to love and care for him.

If your pet is lost or stolen, gather together your family and friends and start searching as soon as you realize your pet is missing. Call the appropriate agencies—animal control, humane society, and your veterinarian. If your pet is wearing a rabies tag or is microchipped, the ID number can be traced to your veterinarian. If you believe your pet has been stolen, call the police and report the incident. Visit your local shelter on a daily basis. Check with your neighbors and place signs in your neighborhood—especially in the area where your pet was last seen.

Oscar

Include a photo and description of your pet, all the telephone numbers where you can be reached, and how long your pet has been missing. Contact your local newspaper and place a "lost pet" ad with them. Check the newspaper daily for notices about "found pets."

Many pet owners have found it helpful to have some type of ceremony or service in memory of the pet. Others have made donations to animal-related causes, veterinary schools, humane societies, or kennel clubs as a memorial to the pet.

> Our 150-pound English mastiff was bitten by a coral snake in our backyard. Despite a mad race to the vet's office, a frantic and successful search to locate anti-venom, and a shot administered within 45 minutes, Guy died 24 hours after the attack.
>
> Within a few weeks, our small town newspaper ran an article on poisonous snake bites on the front page of the local section. A significant portion of the article was about Guy's death. When a dog as large as many men dies from a snake bite, that's news. When that bite occurs in a backyard of a suburban home, that's news—even in our coastal Florida town.
>
> We have had many dogs in the past 30 years, and inevitably old age or illness claimed them all. We are agreed that no grief about a loss of our beloved pets was more devastating than this.
>
> We received over 50 condolence cards, many phone calls, and numerous donations to the Humane Society. The horrifying nature of the death and the resulting newspaper coverage undoubtedly contributed to the response.

The depth and warmth of our community's compassion was uplifting. It has been over two years now, and the grief is still present. There are moments when each of us is pierced by pain. We don't speak about it for fear of hurting each other.
—*Susan Braunstein, personal communication*

THE STORY OF OTIS

The best one word description for Otis, our beloved three-and-a-half-year-old Australian Shepard, was quirky. He was, as most Aussies are, highly intelligent, active, and very eager to please his chosen humans. His unique "quirky" personality developed as he seemed to emulate the very traits that we ourselves possess. Of course, included in the mix was his own special brand of dog wisdom and attitude; add to this the fact that Otis was the runt of his litter, which made him feel he had something to prove. He had to run faster, jump higher, and herd better than any of his peers. Otis had incredible spirit.

Physically, Otis was a beautiful dog. His coat was luxurious, thick, and jet black, with a snow-white chest and nose. In the right light his coat glistened with blue highlights and was as soft as human hair. He had expressive brown/black eyes that could speak volumes in their silence. His smile was an endearing snaggle-toothed grin that would melt our hearts and invariably allow him to have his way with both my husband Casey and me.

Aussies usually have a strong instinctive desire to herd, and Otis was no exception. In fact, it was this desire coupled with a keen curiosity that eventually led to his death. At every opportunity Otis would escape, slipping through the woods to a nearby horse corral to fine-tune his herding skills. This had become a source of concern for both Casey and me, but short of confining him to the house, there was no denying him these mini-adventures.

Although we did not witness the actual event, we pieced together a likely scenario. Otis probably scooted under the corral fence and proceeded to herd a very agitated and unwilling horse. The horse, pushed to his limit, turned and delivered a powerful kick, which landed just above Otis' right eye.

After a traumatic emergency visit to the veterinarian's office, we were sent home to try and nurse Otis through the night. A number of hours into the ordeal we both began to realize that he might not survive. The swelling became severe and his cries more constant. Certainly, the humane thing to do at that point would have been to end his misery.

Neither Casey nor I could bring ourselves to do it; we were paralyzed and helpless. Despite his pain, Otis managed to wag his little nub of a tail several times when we spoke to him. It was heartbreaking, and it also sparked the hope that perhaps somehow, through some miracle that had been granted to our anguished prayers, he would survive. Otis did not survive. Around 5:00 a.m., after a terrible night filled with misery and suffering, he left us. We buried him in the dark, in the rain, near a cluster of trees and beautyberries. We trudged back to the house in a daze, wet and muddy, and hopelessly distraught, left with the guilt of being too weak to end his suffering, and with the awful, awful pain of losing him.

At some point later in the day I panicked when I realized that I should have clipped a lock of his fur. After choking down the torrent of tears this new thought brought me, I decided to search the house for errant hairballs. The fact that we had been dog-sitting Raven, a very large and very sweet fur bomb of a dog, complicated this task. I embarked on a painstaking mission of collecting and examining individual dog hairs to make certain I had collected only Otis' hair. Exhausted, I sank into the sofa with my zip-lock sandwich bag containing a few precious, silken hairs. It was then that I realized I hadn't showered, hadn't even changed out of my muddy clothes. It was 3:00 in the afternoon and I was a tear-stained, dirty, unshowered, bad-breathed, sleep deprived, quivering mess sitting on the sofa with a sandwich bag of carefully selected dog hairs. It was a desperate and slightly ridiculous moment for me, but finally after yet another torrent of tears, I showered and crawled into bed, if not consoled, at least clean.

The following days were a blur of tears and memories that Casey and I shared with each other. Family and friends dropped in to pay their respects bringing flowers and cards and offering comfort. My parents gave us a red rose bush to plant at his grave, red to signify their love for Otis. In fact it was comforting to know that Otis had been important to others, that he had left an impression on many people.

The pain is still fresh; it hasn't been so very long ago that Otis died. The tears are still a frequent part of life, I still expect to feel his hot breath on my face as he says good morning every day, I still expect him to bound into bed with us every night for "snuggle-time" before taking up his position at the bedroom door, and most of all I still want to squeeze him and kiss his little head and tell him I love him. He was, he still is, exceptional.

—*Rose M. Wood, personal communication*

LYING IN THE ROAD

Suddenly the feeling that this was all just a dream ended. Christopher was angry. It wasn't fair. Why did that dumb man have to hit Bodger?

"I ought to run him over with a truck."

"Oh, honey, Bodger ran right in front of him. The man didn't have time to stop."

They took Christopher home to bed where he relived the accident over and over in his mind. He tried to pretend that the truck had missed the dog, or that he hadn't called and Bodger had stayed on the other side. Or he pretended that they hadn't left the dirt road, where there were hardly any cars. Or that they had stayed home and waited.

But the bad dream always rolled on, out of his control until the moment when Bodger was lying in the road.

—Carol Carrick. The Accident *(1976)*
Seabury/Clarion, New York, p. 3.

TEYRO

Being from a large family, we had lots of pets. Everyone had their own favorite. We had dogs, cats, parrot, fish, and geese. My pet was a dog I named Teyro. He was an ordinary dog, little and scrawny because he was the last and weakest of a litter. He became my favorite because the others ignored him and he clung to me for his needs and comfort. I was ten years of age and all I could think of was that he was the most beautiful dog in the whole wide world and I had to take care of him.

In my country (Trinidad) 43 years ago, I was not aware of the different breeds of dogs and my Teyro was called a pot hound. He grew up to be a huge brown with black spotted dog, with a quiet and loving nature. Teyro followed me wherever I went, which was mostly around the yard and house since I was not allowed to go outside the gate without someone older and responsible.

Teyro had a habit to walk out of the yard to go potty by himself, and one day when I was at school, he took the opportunity to come look for me after he was done pottying. While crossing a busy intersection he was knocked down by a truck. My parents were called and Teyro was taken home for treatment. In Trinidad, most families took care of their pet's injuries since vets were not as common as today. Teyro's right leg was broken, so my parents thought, since there was an open wound. Both my parents looked after him. His wound was healing but Teyro's spirit for survival was missing, or so I thought. My parents told me he was old and that he needed more time to heal. Later I was told he was not old (only five years old), but it was a way my parents tried to make it easy for me to take the end result.

Teyro stopped eating and for a while he was fed through a nipple bottle with egg-enriched milk. He eventually stopped eating and soon after he died. I remember saying that he was not dead, but only asleep, and I forbid them from burying him. I later realized that he was no more and we buried him in his favorite corner of the yard. He was buried in a wooden box made by my father and lots of flowers were put on his grave. For a while, it was a daily routine that I would sit by his grave pretending he was alive and that he was out pottying. My parents became very concerned about my mood and they took action. My mother kept me busy in the kitchen. She taught me to cook, bake, and even to sew with my hands, while my father kept me and the other kids busy with games, homework, and other tiring exercises. I would say both my parents supported me well through this time.

After Teyro died we had many dogs but I would not get close to them. I pretended that I was afraid of them, so I would not have to play, feed, or give any attention to them. Because of my pretending, I am now slightly afraid of dogs. I will pet them but I am always on the defense, ready to react to them.

Losing my pet dog, Teyro, has changed me. When my kids ask for a dog as a pet, I try and discourage them. I really do not want them to go through the loss and pain of losing a pet. I know it is selfish, but that is how I feel.

—Taramati Sahib-John, personal communication

CHAPTER 3

When a Pet is Euthanized

> To every thing there is a season, and a time to every purpose under the heaven: a time to be born and a time to die.
> —*Ecclesiastes iii, 1*

Your relationship with your pet is a special one, and you are responsible for its care and welfare. Eventually, we are faced with making life or death decisions for our pets. This decision may become necessary for the welfare of the pet as well as for you and your family. The kindest thing you can do for your pet when it is extremely sick or so severely injured that it will never recover normal health is to have your veterinarian induce its death quietly and humanely through euthanasia. Euthanasia literally means "gentle death." Other euphemisms (or terms) you may hear are "put to sleep," "put down," "put out of its misery," or, less kindly, "destroy." The decision to have your pet euthanized is a serious one and seldom easy to make.

A frequently asked question is, "When is the right time to euthanize my pet?" The veterinarian is the best judge of your pet's physical condition; however, you are the best judge of the quality of your pet's daily life. If a pet has a good appetite, responds to attention, seeks its owner's company, and participates in play or family life, many owners feel that this is not the time to euthanize their pet. However, if a pet is in constant pain, undergoing difficult and stressful treatments that aren't helping greatly, unresponsive to affection, unaware of its surroundings, and uninterested in life, a caring pet owner will probably choose to end the pet's suffering. Remember what your animal's personality and lifestyle were when she was fully well. Perhaps it was a cat that was very fond of a special toy or a dog that loved to run around and play. If those activities that the animal used to relish now hold little pleasure—or cause pain—perhaps it is time to weigh quality of life against quantity. If your pet cannot respond to you in the usual ways, you may need to consider euthanasia. If your pet is seriously ill or injured, euthanasia may be a valid option. I would advise communicating with your pet and try to understand what she is telling you. We can pick up on pain through a glassy stare or a cloudy look. When responses begin to distress you, attempt to look deeper. You may see a faraway expression in the eyes, as if she is already close to death. To help you prepare for the decision to euthanize your pet, consider the following ten questions. They are intended as a guide, for only you can decide what is best for your pet.

1. What quality of life does your pet currently have?
2. Is your pet eating well?
3. Is your pet still playful?
4. Is your pet affectionate toward you?
5. Is your pet interested in the activity going on around it?
6. Is your pet tired a lot of the time?
7. Does your pet seem withdrawn most of the time?
8. Is your pet in pain?
9. Is there anything you can do to make your pet more comfortable?
10. Are there any alternative treatment options available?

We must consider the dignity of our animal friends. Remember that animals are proud. To some, the sense of self-esteem that goes along with protecting you or using the litter box independently is paramount. The relationship with your beloved pet has always been one of mutual respect and you must honor that to the end.

Sometimes the reason for euthanasia may be a financial or emotional cost. If this is the case, strongly consider discussing this situation with your veterinarian. Other arrangements may be made such as alternative methods of payment and grief counseling. Your veterinarian understands attachment to pets and can examine and evaluate your pet's condition, estimate your pet's chances for recovery, and discuss potential disabilities and long-term problems. He or she can explain the medical options and possible outcomes. Since it is your responsibility to make the euthanasia decision, it is important that you fully understand your pet's condition. If there is any part of the diagnosis or the ramification for your pet's future that you don't understand, ask to have it explained again.

Unfortunately, there may be a situation where your pet has become dangerous, vicious, or unmanageable, and euthanasia is recommended.

Remember, some undesirable and abnormal behaviors can be changed. Economic, allergies, or changes in living conditions also may force one to consider euthanasia of a pet, but it is much better to find another solution or an alternative home for the pet. Euthanasia should be the last resort in the above-mentioned cases—when there is no other alternative.

Telling other family members may be a concern to you. In many cases, the family is already aware of a pet's condition. However, you should discuss with them the information you have received from the veterinarian. Long-term medical care can be a burden that you and your family may be unable to bear emotionally or financially. This should be talked about openly and honestly with everyone involved. Even if you have reached a decision, it is important that family members have their feelings considered—especially the children. Children often feel a strong attachment to their pets. They are friends, confidants, and good buddies. Their loss is a significant one and should not be minimized. Not including them in this discussion may only complicate their grieving. Involving a child in the experience of a pet's death through discussion and ritual provides an excellent learning experience as well as a means of coping with the loss. What is helpful in healing is acknowledging the loss as a loss. It is important to create a ritual of good-bye—burying the pet in a special place. The ritual might include a song and a wooden marker.

Although making the decision to part with a pet is certainly an emotional one, it can also be a peaceful experience. It is an agonizing scene when the bond between humans and animals is suddenly under threat. We feel out of control and lost—not knowing where to turn. When the doctor says, "It's time," we feel a sense of relief—the struggle of making the decision alone has ended.

Another concern is the pain that might be involved in euthanasia. Understanding how the procedure is performed may be helpful in deciding on euthanasia as a choice and whether the family wishes to be present during the procedure. Initially, a pet is made as comfortable as possible. Some veterinarians will perform the procedure in a pet's home. If the animal is brought to the hospital, veterinarians often choose a quiet room where the pet will feel more at ease. Sometimes a mild sedative or tranquilizer is first given if the animal appears anxious or in pain. Euthanasia is usually accomplished by injection of an anesthetic overdose into the vein of a foreleg. It is injected into the pet's vein to ensure that the euthanasia solution is delivered quickly. The solution is usually a barbiturate—the same class of drugs used for general anesthesia. In elderly or sick animals where the veins have collapsed, the injection may be made into a kidney or the heart. Sometimes a catheter is placed to allow easy access to the veins. As the solution is injected, the animal loses consciousness. Within minutes the heart and lungs stop functioning. Since the pet is not conscious, it does not feel anything. Death comes quickly and painlessly. Most times, the animal dies so smoothly that it is difficult to tell until the veterinarian listens for absence of a heartbeat. If you are holding your pet, you will feel him exhale, relax, and become heavier in your arms. Urine may trickle from his bladder as the muscles relax. This is completely normal and is something an owner should expect. In addition, after death, chemicals normally stored in nerve endings are released causing occasional muscle twitching in the early post-mortem period. Many owners who choose to stay with their pets are surprised how quickly and easily the pet is put down. Most vets will place the animal into a natural looking sleeping position and close his eyes since animals do not always close their eyes when they die. Because all the muscles of the face have relaxed, his lips may pull back into what looks like a grimace. This is simply due to relaxation of the muscles and to gravity and is not a sign of pain, but it can cause concern if you do not expect it. If you have provided a towel or blanket, the vet will normally wrap or cover your pet's body. Otherwise, he may place him in a black bag. This is not a sign of disrespect. It is for hygiene and your own privacy. Most veterinary practices have a place where you can sit for a few minutes afterwards and regain your composure. If you do need a few moments before you are able to leave, tell the veterinarian. Alternatively, someone may be able to help you back to your car, but bear in mind they may not have the time to sit with you. I suggest paying the bill first so that you do not have to linger in the waiting area.

The most important step in the process of euthanasia is saying goodbye to your pet. I strongly consider this as a way to manage the natural and healthy feelings of grief, sorrow, and sense of loss. Your pet is an important part of your life and it is normal to feel you are losing a friend—because you are. Gather the family together for a last evening with your pet—at home or in the hospital. Those who want to be alone with the animal should be allowed to do so. Farewells are always difficult but very, very important. Talk to your pet. Tell him, "I know you are in pain. It is all right to leave me now." Animals seem to understand. Talking to your pet makes it easier to let go.

Another important question regarding euthanasia is "Should I stay during euthanasia?" The decision to stay or not stay with a pet is a very personal one. Some owners feel they should comfort their pet in its final minutes. Many feel this is the ultimate gesture of love and comfort you can offer your pet. Some feel relief and comfort themselves by staying. They were able to see that their pet died peacefully and without pain, and that it was really gone. For many, not witnessing the death (and not seeing the body) makes it more difficult to accept that the pet is really dead. However, on the other hand, this can also be very traumatic. Others feel their emotional upset would only upset their pet. You must ask yourself honestly whether you will be able to handle it. Although uncontrolled emotions and tears are natural, they are likely to upset your pet. Euthanasia is emotional for veterinarians as well. Sometimes, the veterinarian has known the pet for a long time or has tried very hard to make the animal well again. James Herriot stated the view of most veterinarians in *All Things Wise and Wonderful*: "Like all vets I hated doing this, painless though it was, but to me there has always been a comfort in the knowledge that the last thing these helpless animals knew was the sound of a friendly voice and the touch of a gentle hand."

If you are willing to pay a call-out fee, your veterinarian will euthanize your pet in your own home. Both you and your pet may find this less traumatic than waiting at the clinic. You must decide what will be least traumatic for you and your pet, as well as for other members of your family. Discuss your desires and concerns with your veterinarian. If he or she is not able to accommodate your wishes, then request a referral.

SHELLIE

My beloved Shellie, my pet for 15 years, passed away on April 12, 2001. Shellie was a miniature poodle who gave me great joy and happiness. She was my pal, my best friend. Last year, Shellie started going blind and was losing her hearing. As the months went on, Shellie was starting to move slowly, but I was in denial. She was not well and I did not want to take her to the vet fearing I would have to put her to sleep. Needless to say, that day did come.

The emptiness I feel at times is devastating and my final memories of her seem too hard to bear. My husband cried, too, while I was sobbing in his arms at the vet's office. We knew this day would come, but didn't want it to come. She was part of our family and it is such a great loss. You don't realize how much a pet is a part of your life until they are gone.

Through support of my husband, son and daughter, my family, and my dearest friends, I have been able to grieve. I am still not over the loss of Shellie, and while writing this letter, it has been very hard for me to hold back the tears.

There is such emptiness in the house, something is missing, and the thought of getting another dog doesn't sit well with me. I would love to have another dog/companion some day, but I am still not ready to do that yet. I feel like no other dog could every replace my Shellie.

My husband and I picked a spot in the backyard where we buried Shellie's remains and planted some plants to make a small memorial. That has made me feel better knowing that she is home and will always be with us.

—*JoAnn Scamorza, personal communication*

BAMBI

My sister's dog gave birth to a litter and my wife and I took one of the pups. We named her "Bambi" and had her for 13 years. She was an affectionate, well-behaved dog. She went on vacations with us to Florida, Canada, and Cape Cod. She was a wonderful traveler. In her 15th year, she contracted cancer and became paralyzed in her back legs. We had to put her to sleep. It was like losing a member of the family. It took years to get over the loss of Bambi. We decided not to get another pet as we didn't want to go through the sorrow again.

—*Harry A. Karcher, personal communication*

Bambi

A Dog Named Spike

I would like to tell you about a dog named Spike
Who everyone he met he seemed to like.
His fur was as white as January snow
And wherever it would fall that's where he liked to go
When I first had found him he was so fluffy and small
But that didn't last long for he soon grew big and tall.
Everyone would say, "What a big dog was he"
But he always seemed to be a puppy to me.
He liked to go for walks or rides in the car
No matter if the travel was near or far.
And if he was sick or in any pain
He never seemed to frown or complain.
No matter the time or the place
He always seemed to have a smile on his face.
But now, Spike has gone away
And I miss him more every single day.
He holds a special place in my heart
From my memory he will never part.
His eyes so gentle the way he greeted me at the door
A better friend, I could never ask for.
I will never forget the joy he had brought
And the lessons in life he seemed to have taught.

Spike

To take so little but give so much away
That is the best way to make it through each day.
And so in closing there is nothing I would better like
That you would also remember "A dog named Spike."
—Robert Olechowski, personal communication

MICKEY

Mickey, my angel, is in heaven now. I took him to the vet—it was time. He could not walk at all and I had been force-feeding him for over three weeks. He was the love of my life for 16½ years and I miss him so much.

—Jane Rasmussen, personal communication

ALEX

Alex was born on New Year's Day in 1996 and everything about him reflected what you would expect from a New Year's baby. His happy go lucky personality and loving disposition is something that my wife and I will remember for years to come. So how do you come to know such a wonderful friend?

A little over six years ago, I called a veterinary friend of mine to ask for some assistance finding a Golden Retriever puppy. He quickly told me to skip the puppy stage; he had a 10-month-old Golden that needed saving at the humane society. That afternoon I met Mr. Scooter. I guess you could say it was love at first sight. The only exception was his name, Scooter. It sounded too much like how a dog would scratch himself. I guess you get the picture. Bottom line, he just looked like an Alex. Everything was large about our boy. He had big brown eyes, a big smile, but most of all a big heart. The funny thing about him was the way he would wink at you almost to say, "Yep, I understand, no more digging in the yard. I can do that." It's my understanding Alex was not always so mellow. The gang at the Humane Society forgot to inform me of Alex's nickname, "The Dog from Hell." It seems they had a small problem the day they went to pick him up. Nothing big, he just decided to eat the inside of their van. So here I was with a new truck and a new dog that was born in one of the hotter regions of our universe. I was a little nervous to say the least. However, like most things, this was a lesson in why we should not worry about the small things. Mr. Alex jumped in the truck. I plugged in a Jimmy Buffett CD. Mr. Alex laid his head on the console and never moved the whole way home. I found out that day he was not from the land down under. Alex was born in Margaritaville.

After six wonderful years, we started to notice that Alex was starting to lose weight. Not wanting to take any chances, Ginny took him to our veterinarian right away. It was determined that he had a bladder infection and with a couple of weeks of antibiotics and a little love he'd be just fine. This was on Thursday, June 27th. Throughout the weekend, we tried everything we could to get Alex to eat. Finally, I scrambled some eggs and fed him from my hand. At this point, we knew something was seriously wrong. With the exception of being brushed, Alex's favorite thing in life was eating. I took Alex back to the vet on Tuesday morning, July 2nd. In that short four-day period, his red blood count was cut in half and his platelets went from 72 to 22. Our veterinarian was amazed. We immediately ordered toxic screen tests for every type of tick and disease she could think and then took a chance by putting him on steroids and more antibiotics. Alex stayed the night and showed major improvements by Wednesday afternoon. For all indications, it looked like we were on the right track. Alex continued to grow stronger and his appetite was growing with leaps and bounds. By the afternoon of the 4th of July, he was swimming in the pool and playing with our granddaughter. This improvement was a shot in the arm for the whole family.

The 4th of July, 2002, is a day my wife and I will never forget. That night Alex started getting sick. At first, we thought he had just overdone it but his condition continued to worsen throughout the night. The final and last thing to do was exploratory surgery. My sister, wife, and I stayed with Alex until it was time for him to head to the operating room. Alex kept looking at us as if he was asking for help. To date, I have never felt so useless. This guy gave us unconditional love and with all the medical knowledge of both our veterinarians, we still could not make him comfortable. But, like always, Alex did it for us. All at once, he rose up his head and gave us a big wink as to say, "Don't worry, Dad. Everything's going to be just fine."

An hour into the surgery we got the phone call from both our vets. Alex's spleen and liver were huge. Neither one, in all their years of practice, had witnessed a spleen or liver of this proportion. It was time for some hard decisions to be made. The only thing left to do was to wait and see what would happen. Alex had a 20 percent chance of waking up, and if he did, the pain would be unbearable. We asked our vet not to wake Alex up. He was too good of a friend to let suffer.

I lost my mother to a brain aneurysm. Our family had to make the decision to turn off the life support system. This is something I would not wish on anybody. Now, with my wife, we had made the decision to let our best friend die in peace. If you have or will have to make this decision, I hope you can take comfort in something my father said to me when I called him about Alex. In Dad's normal common sense way he simply said, "Jim, wouldn't you want us to do the same thing if it was you that was suffering?" Once again, he was right. If I were suffering like Alex, I am hopeful that someone would help me out. Losing a loved one is never easy. I guess it is just part of living. We're born, we live, and we die. All we can control is how we live each day. God bless you.

—*Jim and Ginny Comer, personal communication*

DAISY

I used to have a lady called Daisy. I found her when I was on a temporary assignment to haul chemicals for McKensie Truck Lines. Whenever I returned to the yard with my rig (10,000 gallon tanker), she would run around my truck as soon as I turned into the yard. I gave the pup my sandwich just because I was just too busy to eat it myself. I was a lot skinnier then. She did the, "I love you and your truck thing" for three weeks. It is not healthy to run around 65 tractor trailers just to find the one truck who likes you. The animals make it look easy. As soon as I pulled into the yard, the only thing that differentiated me from all the other trucks was the #63. And, of course, my good looks helped! It wasn't just the sandwich that I gave her every day—it was the "I am so happy to see you again emotion." I took her home, and she peed in my car on the way. Anticipation, just had to go, or just happiness? Well, since that time she has been with me and lived 13.45 years more. She was my love and sweetie. She was never really sick where the doctor could not help until she got older. She developed a stomach cancer that made her bleed. She was embarrassed about it, and I could tell. I personally took care of her until I asked the family veterinarian to please tell me "Now what?" She knew how attached I was to Daisy and told me that she could do surgery with 30 percent chance of improvement. I spent many, many, many hours thinking about the right decision and decided to do the lethal injection. The day I did the second or third hardest thing in my life, I held her and hugged her and kissed her when the doctor injected her. She looked at me, and trusted me. I loved her so much.

—*Jim McCabe, personal communication*

His Apologies

Master, this is Thy Servant. He is rising eight weeks old.
He is mainly Head and Tummy. His legs are uncontrolled.
But Thou hast forgiven his ugliness, and settled him on Thy knee...
Art Thou content with Thy Servant? He is very comfy with Thee.
Master, behold a Sinner! He hath committed a wrong.
He hath defiled Thy Premises through being kept in too long.

Wherefore his nose has been rubbed in the dirt and his self-respect
  has been bruised.
Master, pardon Thy Sinner, and see he is properly loosed.
Master, again Thy Sinner! This that was once Thy Shoe,
He has found and taken and carried aside, as fitting matter to chew.
Now there is neither blacking nor tongue, and the Housemaid has us
  in tow,
Master, remember Thy Servant is young, and tell her to let him go!
Master, extol Thy Servant, he has met a most Worthy Foe!
There has been fight all over the Shop—and into the Shop also!
Till cruel umbrellas parted the strife (or I might have been choking
  him yet),
But Thy Servant has had the Time of his Life—and now shall we call
  on the vet?
Master, behold Thy Servant! Strange children came to play,
And because they fought to caress him, Thy Servant went away.
But now that the Little Beasts have gone, he has returned to see
(Brushed—with his Sunday collar on) what they left over from tea.
Master, pity Thy Servant! He is deaf and three parts blind.
He cannot catch Thy Commandments. He cannot read Thy Mind.
Oh, leave him not to his loneliness; nor make him that kitten's scorn.
He hath had no other God than Thee since the year that he was born.
Lord, look down on Thy Servant! Bad things have come to pass.
There is no heat in the midday sun, nor health in the wayside grass.
is bones are full of an old disease—his torments run and increase.
Lord, make haste with Thy Lightnings and grant him a quick
  release!

—Rudyard Kipling

BUSTER

Our children, Johnnie and Jenifer, were 11 and 8 respectively at the time of the adoption. My husband Marvin and I had waited to acquire a family pet until we thought the kids were both old enough to participate actively in its care.

A Cocker Spaniel or Dachshund were on our list of preferred breeds, so when we learned that there was a Cocker Spaniel available for adoption, Jenifer and I made a trip to the Humane Society. After arriving at the kennel, we were saddened to learn that the staff had determined that particular Cocker Spaniel was not suitable for adoption into a family with young children. Jenifer, as many 8-year-old girls are prone to do, immediately broke into tears. One of the staff members suggested that we tour the kennel anyway because there were several other dogs that were believed to be excellent candidates for adoption by a family such as ours. Begrudgingly, we agreed to take the tour.

The room was terribly noisy with its concrete floor, cement block walls, and open rafter ceiling. Two large fans, one in the rafters and one on the floor at the end of the aisle, hummed as we slowly walked down the aisle between cages. We paused at each gate to read the card that detailed breed, gender, estimated age, etc. of each dog. The first dog was way too big, the next was mean looking, another stood at his gate and yapped in a shrill and annoying voice. Disappointment about the Cocker Spaniel seemed to cloud our enthusiasm for any of the other animals.

Not overly concerned about reading the details on the cards, Jenifer had moved along a little faster than I did. She suddenly stopped at a cage a few feet in front of where I was then standing. Motioning to me, she called out, "Mom, come quick! Look at this one!" There at the gate stood a little white fuzzy ball of a dog that the staff had temporarily named Cracker. He had short legs and a fairly long body like a Dachshund or Pekinese, but he definitely had a really bad fuzzy poodle hairdo! He made no sound as he looked up through the chain link fencing with his big brown eyes. Instead, he spoke to us silently, but ever so cheerfully as his whole body wiggled back and forth in time with the motion of his tail. When Jenifer bent down to near floor level, he stuck his pink tongue out through the chain links and gently licked the back of her hand.

The staff member escorting us suggested that we leash him and take him out to the grassed play area to see how he responded to us. She warned us that he might simply run around once the leash was removed. Instead, he walked over to Jenifer and leaned his snout up against her little sandaled foot. "Look Mom, I think he loves me already!" Thus, it came about that the Rhoden family adopted a dog. Not the dog that we went after, but the one that appeared to know us and love us right from the start.

When we pulled into our driveway later that afternoon, Johnnie ran out of the house to met us. Viewing the little dog for the first time, his first words were, "No way! That's a girly looking dog!" Trying to dispel his disappointment at our having not brought home something a little more ferocious, I said, "Tell you what . . . you can name him. That way you can pick a manly name!"

There were two professional heavyweight boxers back then that held Johnnie's fascination, Mike Tyson and Buster Douglas. A family friend had recently named their new dog Tyson, so he said that name was out of the question. With a twinkle in his eye he announced, "We'll play with the words and officially name him Buster Dogless instead of Douglas, but we'll just call him Buster!" Buster is a name that is typically associated with masculinity and fearlessness. Not so our Buster! He was as prissy as they come. He especially disliked walking in the dewy wet grass in the morning, and he was so frightened by rainstorms that he'd run and hide under the bed with the first rumble of thunder even if it was way off in the distance.

Over the years, Buster became very much a fifth member of our family. He learned to tolerate each of our idiosyncrasies as much as we did his. Thanksgiving, Christmas, and Easter meals seemed to be some of Buster's favorite times. Just the sound of Marvin starting up the electric carving knife was enough to stop Buster in his tracks and send him into the kitchen to sit and beg for little bits of turkey or ham scraps.

On one family vacation, Buster traveled with us by car to Indiana and stayed at Grandma and Grandpa's house right along with the rest of us. On a particularly sad return trip to Indiana some years later, Buster seemed to sense that something was wrong before we even got there. He walked into the house and laid down on the floor right in front of Grandpa's chair, but Grandpa would never again sit in that chair, or any other chair for that matter.

I've shared all of this with you so that you'd have a better understanding of how difficult it was for us when, 12 years after the adoption, we had to consider Buster's impending death. He was very sick, and there was no hope for his improvement, but none of us really dared to speak of it. As Christmas approached and we finalized our plans for a family holiday vacation to Indiana, Marvin and I discussed what we could or should do about Buster. After talking to the staff at the vet's office, we decided that we'd board him there the day before we were scheduled to leave town and that we'd ask the doctor to relieve him of all his pain and suffering while we were out of town. It might seem silly to some, but I cried through most of the phone call. The plans were made, but the thought of Buster leaving this world while lying on a cold metal table in the care of strangers was still almost more than we could talk about. If only there was another way. But what?

After having worked through Buster's death, I trust now even more that God really is merciful and that he loves each one of his creatures—the big ones, the small ones, the human ones, and yes, the animal ones! Three days before Buster was scheduled to be dropped off at the vet, Marvin called me at work shortly after I arrived there. "What are we going to do about Buster?" he wondered. I asked, "What do you mean?" I quickly ran through the plans including the part about picking him up when we returned so that we could bury him at home. But he said, "No, he's gone." Marvin told me that after their morning walk together around the backyard, that Buster had a seizure on the family room floor while Marvin was reading the newspaper close by. Marvin had picked Buster up and held him in his arms as he tried to comfort him. Buster's heart beat, **beat**, **beat**, **harder** and **faster**, **harder**, and **faster**, as time ticked by and the seizure continued. After just a few minutes, Buster turned his head and looked toward Marvin's face. He blinked his eyes one time, and then closed them forever. God is compassionate and he cares about all of his creatures. Buster died, not on a cold metal table surrounded by strangers, but in the warm and comforting arms of someone who loved him. And Marvin or I didn't have to suffer through the experience of leaving Buster at the vet to be put to sleep.

It's been almost a year and a half since Buster left us and it has taken all this time for me to be able to put his story to words. I'm finally at the point that I can talk and laugh about the good times we had with him and the funny things he did over the 12 years he was a member of the family. From time-to-time, small patches of wild flowers sprout up and grace several areas of our yard near where Buster is buried. Some were in bloom the other day, and as I gazed at their unassuming beauty through the porch screen, I smiled to myself as a brief image of Buster in his better, younger days flashed through my mind. As I reflected on their simple beauty, I realized that those few wild flowers were serving as a special reminder to me that life blooms and then dies off in its own due time. I don't really understand it. I don't think I'm supposed to. But when I allowed myself to pause for just a minute to contemplate the beautiful things and loving people that surround me on a daily basis, a special peace of mind and happiness surfaced from a place deep within me that once could only call up what seemed to be an infinite sadness.

—Donna M. Rhoden, personal communication

The Last Battle

If it should be that I grow frail and weak and pain should keep me
   from my sleep,
Then will you do what must be done? For this—the last battle—can't
   be won.
You will be sad I understand, but don't let grief then stay your hand,
For on this day, more than the rest, your love and friendship must
   stand the test.
We have had so many happy years, you wouldn't want me to
   suffer so.
When the time comes, please, let me go.
Take me to where my needs they'll tend, and only, stay with me till
   the end.

Hold me firm and speak to me until my eyes no longer see.
I know in time you will agree it is a kindness you do to me.
Although my tail its last waved, from pain and suffering I have been saved.
Don't grieve that it must be you who has to decide this thing to do.
We've been so close—we two—these years; don't let your heart hold any tears.

—Author Unknown

Farewell, Master, yet not farewell.
Where I go, ye too, shall dwell.
I am gone before your face,
A moment's time, a little space.
When ye have come where I have stepped
Ye will wonder why ye wept.

—Author Unknown

CHAPTER 4

Telling the Children

> There is only one smartest dog in the world, and every boy has it.
> —*Anonymous*

The death of a cherished pet may be the very first loss a child experiences and may be most painfully felt, as will any first encounter with death and bereavement. Although such animals as dogs, cats, and horses are most likely to affect the child, even the deaths of goldfish and turtles can be significant. If this pet has been a valued source of attachment, the child is likely to grieve and mourn for it. Many people do not realize how traumatic and confusing death can be for a child. Although children tend to grieve for shorter periods of time, their grief is no less intense than that experienced by adults. Children also tend to come back to the subject repeatedly, so extreme patience is required when dealing with the grieving child.

If your pet's death is imminent, you can talk about feelings before your pet's demise. Depending on the ages of your children, tell them what you can about the pet's illness and tell them that death will occur. Children may not know what euthanasia means, but communicating that, "We're going to help Niggy die so he won't be in any more pain" provides an accurate and simple explanation. Include children in memorials and rituals—they usually enjoy planning and participating in ceremonies for their pets. Many express their grief easily through drawings of the pet or writing a letter to the pet. Another way to allow the child to honor their pet is by planting flowers or trees in their memory. Express your feelings to your child and discuss similar experiences you had in your childhood. Listen to your child's feelings. Include your child in the decision-making about terminating the pet's life. This will spare your child bitterness that can last a lifetime.

One of the most difficult times for a parent is when a child is in pain. Perhaps that's why when the family pet dies, it's tempting to try to soften the blow with half-truths like "The cat went to live in a barn where a lot of mice live." When a pet dies, parents may wonder how best to help their child cope with the loss. Should they minimize the child's loss or see it as a natural opportunity for the child to learn what death means? If children don't know why you are sad, they may feel at fault. Parents must be extra-sensitive. How death is explained will differ according to the age of the child. This is one of those teachable moments that can mark an important time in your child's life. Many people report that their first experience of death was with a pet, and how that was handled can set a pattern for how they deal with loss all their lives. People tend to believe that children don't mourn, but they do. They often can't express themselves verbally, so they act out or have regressive behaviors like bedwetting. The following age categories may help you in guiding your child through grief when their beloved pet dies.

Children who are three years of age and under typically have no understanding of death. They often consider it a form of sleep and don't understand the permanency of it. It is very important to explain that Bootsy isn't coming back—no matter what. They should be told that their pet has died and will not return. Never say things like, "God took your pet," the pet "is sleeping," or the pet "ran away." The child will learn to fear that God will take them, their parents, and/or their siblings. The child will be afraid of going to sleep or may spend every waking moment looking for the pet that ran away. The two or three year old should be reassured that the pet's failure to return has nothing to do with what the child has said or done. Usually, a child in this age range will readily accept another pet in place of the former one (Feinman, 1996).

Children from four to six years of age have some understanding of death but in a way that relates to continued existence. The pet may be considered to be living underground while continuing to breathe, eat, and play. To this age group, the pet may be considered asleep. A return to life may be expected if the child views death as temporary. They seem most concerned with why their pet no longer responds to them or moves, and they can also be deeply upset if the parents dispose of the pet's body in a way that seems inappropriate. These children often feel that any anger they displayed may have caused the death. This view should be contradicted because they may also transfer this belief to the death of family members in the past. Some children in this age range also see death as contagious and will begin to fear that their own death (or that of family and friends) is approaching. They should be reassured that their death is not likely to happen for a while. Manifestations of grief often take the form of disturbances in bladder or bowel control, eating, and sleeping. This is best managed by parent-child discussions that encourage the child to express feelings and concerns. Several brief discussions are generally more helpful than one or two prolonged sessions (Feinman, 1996).

The irreversibility of death becomes real to children who are seven to nine years of age. They recognize that animals are very different from people, but their attachment to their pets may be so intense that they will need time and opportunity for grief and coming to terms with the loss. The death of a beloved pet is a real tragedy for the child, and well-meaning adults who try to relieve the child's feelings by promising to buy an immediate replacement or by insisting that "it was only a dog" are denying the reality of the child's feelings. They usually do not personalize death. They don't think it can happen to them. However, some may develop concerns about the death of their parents. They may become very curious about death and its implications. Parents should be ready to respond frankly and honestly to questions that may arise. These children want to know all the gory details related to the death and will ask many questions. Be sure to answer all questions as honestly as possible and provide as much information as you can. Several manifestations of grief may occur in these children, including the development of school problems, learning problems, antisocial behavior, or aggression. Additional withdrawal, over attentiveness, or clinging behavior may be seen. Depending on grief reactions of parents or siblings, it is likely that these signs may not occur immediately but several weeks or months later (Feinman, 1996).

Children between the ages of 10 and 12 years of age generally understand death as natural, inevitable, and universal. Consequently, these children often react to death in a manner very similar to adults. Adolescents also react similarly to adults but many may exhibit various forms of denial. This usually takes the form of a lack of emotional display. Consequently, young people may be experiencing sincere grief without any outward manifestations.

You are the best judge of how much information your children can handle about death and the loss of their pet. Don't underestimate them, however. You may find that, by being honest with them, you may be able to address some fears and misperceptions they have about death. Honesty is important. If you say the pet was "put to sleep," make sure your children understand the difference between death and ordinary sleep. Without this knowledge, children may develop difficulties with sleeping—like the fear of never waking up again. Never say the pet "went away," or your child may wonder what he or she did to make it leave, and wait in anguish for its return. That also makes it harder for a child to accept a new pet. Make it clear that the pet will not come back, but that it is happy and free of pain. Be sure to tell the child's teacher about the pet's death so she will be aware of unusual behavior during this time. This gives the teacher the opportunity to do a project in school related to the death of a pet.

Sit down with your child and talk about what the animal meant to each one of you. Laugh and cry together. Celebrate your pet's life! If you look at death as a way to learn about life, it makes the grief process go more smoothly. Many people seem to adhere to the policy of "get over it and get on with your life," but that's not always healthy or effective. Instead, take the time to say goodbye to your pet and reminisce the good times. There are many ways of coping with your loss. Make a scrapbook that tells stories about the pet. Add your favorite pictures from puppyhood through old age or until death of your pet. There are books for children that you can read to your child to comfort them when they are feeling sad. Remember! In order to help your children you need to acknowledge your own grief.

> Children come to understand the beginning—and the ending—of life as they grow up with pets. Childhood pets teach us responsibility, consideration, loyalty, and unconditional love—the facts of life. Why not the facts of death?
>
> *—Author Unknown*

CHAPTER 5
When the Pet is a Companion

> He prayeth well who loveth well both man and bird and beast.
> —*Samuel Taylor Coleridge*

Loss of an animal companion is often described as a typical experience of childhood, but it can also be of parallel importance to adults. A pet's death can trigger a grief almost as intense as that precipitated by the death of a human (Weisman, 1991). For the growing population of widows, widowers, and single adults who live alone, pets can be their only family member and an important source of companionship.

In addition to serving as sources of unconditional love in the lives of children, adolescents, and young and middle-aged adults, companion animals are objects of care and affection in the lives of many elderly persons. As a consequence of growing old in today's society, we may lose both the opportunity and the means of caring for others and of giving of ourselves. Companion-animal visits sponsored by community volunteers to nursing homes offer residents opportunities for conversation, sensory stimulation, tactile warmth, and ongoing relationships with others (Savishinsky, 1988). The effectiveness of these visits derives in part from the symbolic meanings (fears, hopes, values, and identities) that people attribute to pet animals.

Many elderly people who live alone keep a pet, often an aging pet, for comfort and company. It is also something alive that they can touch and that touches them. It has been found that talking to and stroking a pet promotes relaxation and lowers blood pressure in both the pet owner and the pet (Katcher, 1983). According to Akiyama, Holtzman, and Britz (1986-1987), companion animals are valuable assets to grieving widows, particularly elderly widows, because they provide a reason to live and care while supplying entertainment, unconditional love, and companionship. Furthermore, owners of companion pets experience less depression and psychogenic symptoms than non-owners during the period of bereavement.

With the elderly, there is usually a severe bereavement following the death of a pet. This is most likely to happen when the pet is a primary attachment figure. Sometimes a person who has failed to resolve a previous loss may transfer attachment needs to a pet, which becomes a replacement, or link, to the dead person. For the very isolated and lonely older person, the pet may be the main source and repository of undemanding affection. Whatever the cause, the death of a pet may lead to grief and mourning that requires just as much support and understanding, if not more, as other more obvious losses (Raphael, 1983). When a pet dies, the elderly person may not wish to develop another attachment to a pet.

Companion animals also protect and aid socialization among the elderly and, in recent years, have become familiar mascots in many nursing homes, long-term care facilities, and hospitals. In a variety of settings, pets can relieve loneliness, lower stress levels, increase social interaction, contribute to a sense of purpose, and enhance self-esteem. The loss of this relationship, although often dismissed with insensitive remarks, can represent a major bereavement for an elderly person who may otherwise have only limited social contacts. Similarly, grieving may occur when an older adult is no longer able to care for a pet, cannot pay for expensive veterinary care, must give up the pet when moving to new living quarters, or must have a sick, old animal euthanized. Older adults are also concerned about what will happen to a beloved pet if they should die first.

No matter what age we are, a pet may come to symbolize many things to each of us. It may represent a child yet to be conceived or the innocent child in all of us. It may reflect the ideal mate, loving parent, sibling, or playmate. It is a reflection of ourselves—encompassing all the positive and negative qualities we recognize or lack in ourselves. The pet may be all of these things—alternating from one role to the next on any given day for each family member. So be good to yourself and be in the moment. Relish every feeling and emotion you experience. It is all part of our learning process here on earth.

AMADEUS

I am sitting here today thinking about my best friend. I am going to tell you a little about him, and try to keep a dry eye. The story dates back to July of 1989 when I was afforded the opportunity to try out for the sheriff's office K-9 unit. After a vigorous tryout, I was accepted into this unit and waited anxiously for my dog to come. I call him a dog now because that is all he was; little did I know he would soon be a part of my life that I would never lose. You see, on February 14, 1988, a German Shepherd puppy was born in a small town somewhere in Germany; 16 months later he took an 18-hour flight to the United States. I drove down to Miami airport and was escorted to the loading docks for Lufthansa airline. This is when I was first introduced to my new partner. On the top of the crate the name Amadeus was written. At first I thought it to be somewhat a silly name for a dog; however, it was always said to be a bad omen to change your dog's name, so me being the superstitious person I am, there was no way his name would change. We then came home and went to sleep because the following day brought 16 weeks of intense K-9 training.

I went through K-9 school with six other officers and their partners. The school was tough, and the hours long, but both Amadeus and I grew as a team each and every day. In the beginning of school other officers would laugh at Amadeus because of his name, but their laughs soon turned to feelings of apprehension knowing they had to catch him while in the bite suit. A bite suit is a large burlap jacket and pants, which is worn by the decoy. While in the suit, the decoy will hide in buildings, bushes, cars, etc. The suit is large enough that when a dog makes the apprehension the decoy can slip the bite by pulling whatever extremity was being bit towards the rear of the suit. You normally had enough time to do this just prior to the bite, but sometimes the K-9 came in quicker and harder than you could adjust, and although the suit would not puncture, you would feel a tremendous amount of pressure from the jaws of a police dog. When the school ended, I felt confident that Amadeus and I would work well as a team. Amadeus had excelled in tracking, building searches, and civil aggression, not to mention our bond together was well on its way. There was still one thing missing— Amadeus had not been battle tested. The streets are much different than the controlled environment of training, but his test was soon approaching.

We had been working the streets for about three months with nothing of interest to speak of—that is until one night when a burglary call went out at a local West Palm business. After finding the point of entry Amadeus and I went into the building to search for suspects. I was still unsure how he would act if and when he encountered a suspect who was not wearing the training suit, but as quickly as the thought came into my mind it left, for seconds later I heard a blood-curdling scream coming from the next room. As I went in I saw a man fighting Amadeus. It seemed the harder he hit Amadeus the harder Amadeus bit down. The arrest was made and the man brought out. In an instant all my fears of Amadeus not performing in the street were gone; he was now a warrior.

Working a patrol dog was not always handling calls for service or going after criminals. We would constantly be called upon to attend elementary schools and put on displays, a kind of show and tell if you would. This was very enjoyable because you could see the children's faces light up when the dogs came out of the car. They were so fascinated to see the criminal apprehension using a small bite sleeve, and then were allowed to pet the dogs like they were their own. All of our dogs have wonderful personalities and are able to differentiate work from play. We also had to maintain a high level of excellence, which consisted of yearly certifications, both state and national. The first certification is at the state level, and the top dogs from each agency would continue on to the national level. For the five years and six months I was in the unit, Amadeus and I made it to the national level every year, always placing in the top 15 throughout the nation.

You can see by now the love I have for my partner, and it is because of him that I am able to write this story. I responded to a domestic, and after determining the husband was going to be arrested for domestic battery, a fight ensued between him and me. At that time I had only been a police officer for about five years, and I can honestly say I was in the fight of my life, and soon it was for my life. The man I was trying to arrest was five inches taller, and 50 pounds heavier than me; he had managed to spin around on me, and he had my holster unsnapped trying to pull my gun out. I had already broken both of my hands fighting this man, and was running out of opportunities. I could hear Amadeus trying to get out of the car, but my windows were up. Our agency had recently bought and installed remotes, which are worn on our belts; when the button is depressed the rear door opens allowing our partners to exit. I was able to create enough distance between me and the suspect and then activate the rear door allowing Amadeus to help. When Amadeus made the apprehension in the man's right leg, the man turned his aggression toward him. The man began punching Amadeus in the head so hard I thought he would crack his skull, but the harder he hit him, the harder Amadeus would bite. When the suspect began to choke Amadeus, he released his hold on his leg and moved to the man's arm. I was trying to help Amadeus, but was having trouble with my hands broken; I was able to knock the man down, and with Amadeus's tenacity the man gave up and even began crying. It was soon after when I realized Amadeus had saved my life.

Like everything in life, all good things must come to an end. Such is the case one night while driving east on Southern Boulevard, when a woman failed to stop for a stop sign and pulled into the path of my patrol car. Days after the crash I noticed Amadeus was limping; after x-rays it was learned Amadeus had hip damage and would not be able to continue working as a police dog. Subsequently Amadeus was retired.

I am now out of K-9 and assigned to road patrol as a training officer. Amadeus was expected to live out a normal dog's life and for seven years enjoyed the life of dog biscuits and lounging by the pool. It was toward the end of 1998 that I noticed his health declining. For several months we were in and out of the hospital trying many different medications in attempts to ease the obvious pain he was in. A few days before Labor Day 1999, Amadeus was not able to stand or walk. I had to carry him outside just to use the bathroom, and then back inside. I knew I would have to make one of the toughest decisions of my life. It was the weekend and his doctor was closed, but I was able to reach him at his home. I explained to him what was happening and I would be in his office in the morning to put Amadeus to sleep because I was unable to watch him suffer any longer. After I hung up, I went into the bedroom where he was laying and tried to have him get up and move, but by now he could not move. After squirting some water into his mouth with an eyedropper I left him alone. I was sitting in my family room when my girlfriend noticed Amadeus was lying next to me. He knew he was dying, and forced himself to get up and walk into the room where I was sitting; he lay next to my feet and died. That is when a piece of me died also.

I was unsure how I was going to get through this experience. I knew the time was coming, and I tried to prepare myself for the inevitable, but when it happened, I was devastated. I knew I had to take care of him; I could not just leave him on the floor. My girlfriend, Linda, had been in our lives long enough that she too had grown to love Amadeus. I knew that I had to be strong for both of us, so I showed no emotion. Amadeus was wrapped in a blanket and put in our car where we drove him to the emergency clinic. That was the hardest drive I have ever had to make. It seems the harder you try not to cry, the harder you do. Such was the case during the drive. Once at the clinic I lay not only a police officer to rest, but also my partner. I said my good-byes and left. For days after I was numb. I did not want to eat or speak to anyone; I just wanted to be left alone to grieve. In my stubbornness and inability to show emotion in front of the one I love, I failed as a boyfriend because I left Linda to grieve for herself even though I saw that she was reaching out for me. I felt it was not manly to cry in front of her. This made my grieving period much longer. I feel the death of Amadeus has brought Linda and I closer; she was always there for me when I needed her. She always played by my rules and never pushed me to talk until I was ready.

We have set up a memorial for Amadeus in our family room, which consists of a photo with all of his awards, an urn containing his remains, and a candle, which to me signifies the eternal flame. Since his death, Linda has been trying to bring another pet into our home, but I have been unable to allow it, that is until now. I was on my way home when I drove by the animal shelter. I felt compelled to stop, and when I did I found the cutest eight-week-old Shepherd puppy. I phoned Linda and had her meet me so we could pick out a puppy together. What we wound up with was a puppy we named Mozart after his big brother. I thought by getting another dog I could get some closure since it has been almost two years since the death of Amadeus, but I believe I never will.

In the beginning of my story I said that I would try to keep a dry eye. Well I was unable to do that, and actually I have cried throughout most of this paper—sometimes to the point of tears falling onto the keyboard. When I first took on this assignment, I thought how cool it would be to have Amadeus's story told in a book, but now it really does not matter. What does matter is now you know a little bit about my best friend, for now he is gone.

—John Anderson, personal communication

Tribute to a Best Friend

Sunlight streams through the window pane unto a spot on the floor.
Then I remember, it's where you used to lie, but now you are
    no more.
Our feet walk down a hall of carpet, and muted echoes sound.
Then I remember, it's where your paws would joyously abound.
A voice is heard along the road, and up beyond the hill,
Then I remember it can't be yours; your golden voice is still.
But I'll take that vacant spot of floor and empty muted hall
And lay them with the absent voice and unused dish along the wall.
I'll wrap these treasured memorials in a blanket of my love
And keep them for my best friend until we meet above.
—Author Unknown

They will not go quietly, the pets who've shared our lives.
In subtle ways they let us know their spirit still survives.
Old habits still can make us think we hear them at the door
Or step back when we drop a tasty morsel on the floor.
Our feet still go around the place the food dish used to be,
And, sometimes, coming home at night, we miss them terribly.
And although time may bring new friends and a new food dish to fill,
That one place in our hearts belong to them, and surely always will.
—Author Unknown

CHAPTER 6
The Grief Process

> All who have felt an animal's love are touched by sorrow at its passing.
> —*Author Unknown*

What a wonderful responsibility we take on when we bring a pet into our lives. We provide a loving, safe, and healthy environment for our pets that share everything with us. Pets see us through marriages, divorces, and the birth of children. Pets endure separation and welcome us back as if we had been away forever. They are the best pals we have for accepting us as we are. But one day, that relationship will become one of our losses.

One of the most difficult and important parts of grief and loss is seeking to understand what has happened and that what you are feeling is normal. Your sense of loss may encompass your life and that is all right. You have the right to grieve and you can take as much time as you need. In a busy and demanding world, the trick is to take the time.

As a certified grief counselor, I believe "pet loss" is an area that is often overlooked in grief assessment. It is also neglected as a learning opportunity for teaching children about their first death experience. For many, the loss of a pet cannot be equated to that of a human life, but it is a devastating experience for the childless couple, elderly person living alone, or child. In my profession, I have read a lot of literature, listened to many people, participated in numerous discussions concerning the topic of death, and taught the subject to many college students. I have suffered the loss of numerous family members and friends. Each and every time a beloved pet died, I experienced the pain over and over again. All previous losses seem to surface each time another death occurs. It is often said that one cannot compare animal and human death. The losses are different and cannot be adequately measured. What is important is the relationship with the one that has died—whether they are made of flesh or fur. The bond that attaches people to their pet is often extremely strong—a loyal relationship based on unconditional love.

Owners can become quite attached to their pets, especially if their pet is loving and responsive; therefore, the loss of such a pet can cause grief and distress. Indeed, some pets are often such affectionate and responsive animals that people other than the owner can mourn them. It is possible to care for your pet very much, even if you may not seem aware of it at the time. That is not to say that you might be an uncaring person, merely that animals often are undemanding by nature and it is possible to take their presence in our lives for granted. Quite often it is not until a pet dies that we truly become aware of what we had.

Pets can become great companions, especially to children and to those of advanced years. In the latter case, especially when all the children have left home, pets can be seen as new children and a similar attachment may develop. Unless the relationship interferes with your quality of life, it is perfectly healthy. If the pet takes precedence over many aspects of your life, it may be important to reassess your relationship with it, perhaps with the help of a qualified counselor (Nieburg & Fischer, 1996).

I am truly amazed when people apologize for being upset when their pet dies. We grieve for our family and friends when they die, so why not our pets? After all, they amuse us and comfort us and occasionally annoy us. Pets are always there for us, to protect us from harm and to teach us the true meaning of loyalty and love. In turn, they only expect to be fed, cared for, and loved. When they die, or disappear, we need to express all the sadness and grief we feel inside. Unfortunately, there are not enough people who can understand our grief. Those of us who mourn the death of a pet are usually more generous and empathetic in our expressions of care and concern for others. Too often those we rely on most let us down during our grief simply because they do not understand. We may be fortunate to find other caring and supportive people who have pets of their own and who can share our feelings and sadness.

When a pet dies, often people ask "Am I crazy to hurt so much?" Intense grief over the loss of a pet is normal and natural. Don't let anyone tell you that it's silly, crazy, or overly sentimental to grieve! During the months or years you spent with your pet (even if they were few), it became a significant and constant part of your life. It was a source of comfort and companionship, of unconditional love and acceptance, of fun and joy. So don't be surprised if you feel devastated by the loss of such a relationship. People who don't understand the human/pet bond may not understand your pain. All that matters, however, is how you feel. Don't let others dictate your feelings. What you are feeling is valid and may be extremely painful. But remember, you are not alone. Thousands of pet owners have gone through the same feelings.

The experience of grief varies according to the amount of social support available. For instance, our society allows us to have funerals and memorial services for people, but doesn't often understand such a ceremony for pets and puzzles over people who can't seem to get over the animal's death. The usual process that allows the grieving loved one to confront a loss isn't available. Disenfranchised grief—grief experienced in connection with a loss that is not socially supported or acknowledged through the usual rituals—may be experienced after the death of a pet. In some cases, it is more difficult for people to experience the loss of a pet than a parent or a spouse. One client told me that, "The grief for my mother lasted much longer and was more complicated, but my dog's death had me in tears for five straight days." She said she felt extreme guilt because she didn't cry as much for her mother. According to Sandra Barker (1993), many bereaved pet owners are confused by the level of their grief that often seems more intense than that experienced when human family members have died. She reports that 90 percent of pet owners consider their pets to be family members and that many people feel closer to their pets than to their human family members.

Those grieving the loss of a pet may ask, "How long must I suffer like this?" This is a special time when we need all the help we can get. Usually it will last from several days to several weeks; however, there are still some pet owners who feel it is not really socially acceptable to mourn for a pet as we would for a human. This causes enormous internal conflict and disturbance for them, because they seem to need approval and support to grieve for an animal. Understanding the psychological responses and experiences of grief and mourning that other people have gone through can help us when we are going through this process ourselves. The well-established patterns of our lives are abruptly terminated by the death of a beloved pet. Suddenly, we are left alone and in a state of shock. The problems that arise can seem quite overwhelming. Grief is a process of physical, emotional, social, and cognitive reactions to loss. It is difficult to work through. One needs to be patient with oneself and others experiencing loss.

Sometimes we lose our grip on grief and become completely overwhelmed to the point that our grief becomes what is referred to as "complicated grief" or "exaggerated grief." This kind of reaction is somewhat easy to identify since one's emotions become intensified. We may experience extreme irritability and fatigue or excessive anger and persistent nightmares. Sometimes one may even experience near-hallucinations such as hearing or seeing glimpses of the deceased pet. It is not uncommon, however, for an abnormal response to this post-traumatic stress disorder to be overlooked as something that eventually will go away.

I had one client express her guilt for not being with her dog when it died suddenly. We discussed shock and denial, and the truth began to seep in. She quickly lapsed into a deep depression, during which it became necessary for me to discourage her from committing suicide. Fortunately, after several weeks, she was able to return to work. Recovery was slow because of other stresses in her life at the time of her dog's death. The death of her beloved dog was the trigger mechanism that set her off into shock and denial. Through counseling, my client realized the guilt she was experiencing was the cause of her wish to withdraw from life.

It can take a good deal of time to recover from the emotional impact caused by the loss of a pet, especially (but by no means exclusively) a dog or cat. Most people feel unhappy for a long time after the death of their pet. Some days will be better than others although something may occur that might trigger memories of your deceased pet. Shortly after the death has occurred those memories may provoke tears of sorrow, maybe even feelings of anger or resentment. However, after a while (perhaps a year, maybe a little more or a little less) the memories will become pleasant and the positive experiences you shared with your pet will shine through.

THEORIES ON THE GRIEF PROCESS

Researchers have developed stages and phases of grieving as well as medical analogies to provide us with ways of coping with grief. However, they all fall short because they suggest that we can somehow cope with our grief on a time schedule. When we grieve we often can and do return to a normal living routine, but these theories fail to harmonize with our unique experiences when we are grieving. Instead, they emphasize how alike we are and how predictable we will be during our grief work. We are often told how we ought to grieve—that there is a proper way for us to grieve. Unfortunately, neither theory tells us how long we may have to endure our grief or that we actually have control in our grieving. They tend to forget that the griever is the only one who can actually put the pieces of the puzzle back together and move forward in their life. In contrast to the ideas of stages, phases, and medical analogies, some researchers discuss the challenges that we face when we are grieving and the tasks we need to focus on. Survivors may find peace in the idea that there is a broadly recognized consistency in the overall pattern of grief and mourning. Over the past few decades, various models have been proposed and refined as researchers and theorists attempt to describe more and more accurately how people grieve. Although there are many important theorists and researchers with wonderful contributions to the field of dying and death, I have chosen to look at only a few of the models for the intent of this book.

Sigmund Freud

The grief work theory was introduced by Sigmund Freud (1957) following the mass death and bereavement of World War I. Freud was distressed to discover that nations priding themselves on their highly cultivated civilization could behave so brutally toward one another. From his personal sorrows as well as his observation of widespread grief and mourning, Freud offered the following suggestions regarding grief:

- Grief is an adaptive response to loss. It is not just an expression of emotional pain but a kind of work that must be carried out.
- The work of grief is difficult and time-consuming. One cannot quickly snap back to the earlier pattern of life. This can only be stressful and increase the difficulties in working through grief.
- The basic goal of grief work is to accept the reality of the death and thereby liberate oneself from the strong attachment to the "lost object." We must accept the fact that the loved one is really and truly lost to us. We cannot keep clinging to memory, hope, or fantasy. This acceptance must be accomplished on a deep emotional level.
- Grief work is carried out through a long series of confrontations with the reality of the loss. Survivors must deal with all of the feelings, memories, and daily life encounters that bring to mind their attachment to the deceased.
- The process is complicated by the survivor's resistance to letting go of the attachment. We want to stay in touch with the "lost object" in any way we can. This need impairs our efforts to accept the loss and return to normal life.
- The failure of grief work results in continued misery and dysfunction. Survivors who remain intensely attached to the deceased over a prolonged period of time are considered to be suffering from pathological grief.

Freud's grief work theory filled a major gap at the time that it appeared. Through the years since Freud's theory, grief has been taken more seriously. Whether or not one is convinced by the grief work theory, it still deserves much credit for encouraging sensitive attention to the experiences of bereaved people.

Erich Lindemann

In his landmark study after the tragedy of the Cocoanut Grove Fire in Boston, Erich Lindemann (1944), the pioneer in grief investigation, wrote about acute grief as a normal reaction to a distressing situation. The reaction was marked by a definite syndrome with psychological and somatic symptomatology. Five characteristics of grief were noted:

- somatic distress
- preoccupation with the image of the deceased
- guilt
- hostile reactions
- loss of patterns of conduct

There was also a sixth characteristic noted by people who appeared to border on having pathological reactions—the appearance of traits of the deceased in the behavior of the bereaved, especially the symptoms shown during the last illness.

Lindemann described three stages of grief:

- Shock and disbelief, which is recognizable by the inability to accept the loss and occasionally the absolute denial that the loss has occurred.
- Acute mourning, characterized by acceptance of the loss, disinterest in daily affairs, weeping, feelings of loneliness, insomnia, and loss of appetite. There is an intense preoccupation with the image of the deceased.
- Resolution of the grief process, with a gradual reentry into the activities of daily life and a reduction in preoccupation with the image of the deceased.

"Grief work," a term coined by Lindemann, is a process that requires the expenditure of both physical and emotional energy. It causes the bereaved much difficulty, for they fail to anticipate the physical toll the grief process demands. They usually are not prepared for the intensity of their own emotional reactions and/or do not fully understand the importance of accepting and expressing them. Since others are also unaware, they frequently do not provide the social or emotional support necessary to sustain the bereaved during their grief work. The difficulty involved in grief work goes beyond grieving for the actual person who has died—it is for all of the hopes, dreams, fantasies, and unfulfilled expectations the griever held for that person and their relationship. These are symbolic losses that must also be identified and grieved for. And, to go even further, another major factor in dealing with grief is that loss often causes old issues and conflicts to surface. The power of these reawakened memories can be extremely overwhelming.

John Bowlby

In 1961, John Bowlby presented a theory of grief that differentiated three main phases:

- the urge to recover the lost object
- disorganization and despair
- reorganization

These phases are derived from attachment theory, a theory that suggests there are fundamental reasons for the ways humans react to grief. During the course of healthy development, humans instinctively develop attachments, initially between child and parent and later between adult and adult. As with other forms of instinctive behavior, attachment behavior is mediated by homeostatic systems that are goal directed. The goal of attachment behavior is to maintain certain degrees of proximity to or communication with the person to whom the individual is attached. Attachment behavior is characteristic of many species because it contributes to organisms' survival by keeping the organism in touch with its caretakers, reducing the risk of harm (Bowlby, 1969, 1973, 1980).

Since the goal of attachment behavior is to maintain an affectionate bond, any situation that appears to endanger that bond will elicit action to preserve it. The greater the perceived threat of loss, the more intense and varied the actions will be to prevent it. Adults show the need for attachment when there is danger nearby. For example, citing a study of baboons, Bowlby notes that "Not only infants but adults also when under stress are strongly disposed to cling to a companion. Thus an adult female, when alarmed, clings to the back of her husband or is embraced by him. Conversely, when he is under stress during a fight, a male is likely to embrace one of his wives. . . . The persistence into adult life of patterns of behaviour seen first and at greatest intensity during infancy is found, then, to be a regular species of the behavioral repertoire of other primate species" (Bowlby, 1969, p. 130).

When looking at our early experience of separation, adult grief, then, is very similar in comparison. We have all had the anxiety of separation experiences in our lives, even if these were but fleeting experiences. The depressive state of a bereaved pet owner is a classic parallel to the infant who felt abandoned and vulnerable.

Elisabeth Kübler-Ross

Elisabeth Kübler-Ross (1969) outlined five stages a person moves through when coping with imminent death. These have also been used to identify the grief of individuals after a loss. It is believed that people experience each of these stages to some degree, although not necessarily in a step-wise fashion. The grief process for pet loss has been found to be very similar, although the "bargaining" stage is typically less intense (Barker, 1993).

- Denial—a period of shock that functions as a buffer against the overwhelming reality of the situation and then gradually gives way to less radical defenses
- Anger—a period when blame is directed against the doctor, nurses, and God
- Bargaining—a period in which pleas are made to God or the doctor to forestall the loss
- Depression—a period of deep and intense sadness
- Acceptance—a period of facing death calmly

Colin Murray Parkes

Colin Murray Parkes (1983) believes that three tasks must be accomplished in order for recovery from grief to take place:

- Intellectual recognition and explanation of the loss
- Emotional acceptance of the loss
- Assumption of a new identity

William Worden

William Worden's model (1982) of the "tasks of mourning" is an important contribution to our understanding of the process of coping with loss. As Worden states, "Not everyone experiences the same intensity of pain or feels it in the same way, but it is impossible to lose someone you have been deeply attached to without experiencing some level of pain" (p. 13). This model involves the following four tasks:

- Accepting the reality—we must overcome the temptation to deny or avoid the reality of our loss, fully acknowledge it, and recognize its implications for our life patterns
- Working through the pain—we must find effective means to work through and to express the emotions we experience in the aftermath of loss, rather than avoid, circumvent, or repress them
- Adjusting to a changed environment—we must define new life patterns that adjust appropriately and meaningfully for the fact that the deceased is missing
- Emotionally relocating the deceased and moving on with life—we must free ourselves from our bonds to the deceased in order once again to become involved with other persons. We must find effective means to say good-bye

Therese Rando

Therese Rando (1988) also developed a task-oriented model of bereavement. Her "Six R" processes of mourning are essential for healthy accommodation of any loss. This model consists of the following tasks:

- Recognize the loss—acknowledge and understand the death
- React to the separation—experience the pain; feel, identify, accept, and express the reaction to loss; and identify and mourn secondary losses
- Recollect and reexperience the deceased and the relationship—review and remember realistically; revive and reexperience the feelings
- Relinquish the old attachments to the deceased and the old assumptive world
- Readjust to move adaptively into the new world without forgetting the old—develop a new relationship with the deceased, adopt new ways of being in the world, form a new identity
- Reinvest emotional energy in new persons, things, and ideas

You might have noticed that the Lindemann and Worden theories remain very much under the influence of Freud's grief work approach. For Rando, the grieving person does not have to set aside attachments to the deceased to quite the extent recommended by Lindemann and Worden. Rando's basic message is that we can still keep a cherished memory of our relationship with the lost person while we reconstruct our lives and develop other relationships and activities.

Thomas Attig

Thomas Attig (1996) developed the central idea of grieving as a process of relearning the world. This requires that we relearn physical surroundings and find a new place within them; relearn our relationships with others, including fellow survivors, the deceased, and God; and relearn ourselves, that is, our ways of being who we are. Attig says, "Viewing grieving as relearning gives specific content to the active, task-based idea of grieving and defines the range of activities involved. As we grieve, we actually engage in relearning that is not simply a cognitive affair. Instead, we engage as whole persons as we learn how to be and act in the world that is transformed by our losses. We reshape all facets of our lives" (p. 122).

In *Continuing Bonds* by Klass, Silverman, and Nickman (1996), the authors present data from populations who differ in the origins of their grief. They say that the net effect of all these contributions is to show that the resolution of grief involves a continuing bond that the survivor maintains with the deceased. The authors reexamine the idea that the purpose of grief is to sever the bonds with the deceased in order to free the survivor to make new attachments. They offer an alternative model based on the mourner's continuing bonds with the deceased. It is their belief that survivors hold the deceased in loving memory for long periods, often forever, and that maintaining an inner representation of the deceased is normal rather than abnormal. They believe it is more central to survivors' experience than commonly has been recognized. They suggest that these relationships can be described as interactive, even though the other person is physically absent.

CHAPTER 7

Coping with the Loss of Your Pet

> I look at life as a gift of God. Now that he wants it back I have no right to complain.
>
> —*Joyce Cary*

Our pets live relatively short lives. For many of us who love our pets, their death can affect some of us even more than the death of a relative or friend. Give yourself permission to grieve—only you know what your pet meant to you. At a time when you are experiencing such emotional pain, it is very important that you take care of your body and mind. The body is the vessel of the mind that is now feeling intense emotion. Nurturing your body and mind in the time of grief is very important. The following are some tips on coping with the loss of your pet.

NUTRITION

Eat healthy meals even if your appetite is reduced. Always be sure to drink plenty of liquids—especially water.

SLEEP

Be sure to get at least 6 to 8 hours of sleep daily.

EXERCISE

Get physical. Find a way to let off steam that won't hurt others or get you in trouble. Throw balls at a wall and then run to catch them. Go for a long walk beside a river or stream or someplace else in a natural setting.

COMMUNICATION

Find a good listener. Share your thoughts and feelings with them. Talk to people who can empathize with your grief. If your family or friends love pets, they'll understand what you're going through. Don't hide your feelings in a misguided effort to appear strong and calm. Working through your feelings with another person is one of the best ways to put them in perspective and find ways to handle them. I advise you not to feel shame about showing emotion when your pet dies since the expression of grief is part of mourning. Find someone you can talk to about how much the pet meant to you and how much you miss it—someone whom you feel comfortable with while crying and grieving. Consistent interaction and sharing with those you feel comfortable with is very beneficial. Seek out people who have suffered the loss of a pet—they make the best listeners. Tell someone a relative has died, and you receive a sympathetic hug and a how-can-I-help response. But say that Misty, your cat, has died and the person may be less supportive. "If someone says, "It was just a pet," or "Aren't you over that yet?" avoid them until you're feeling stronger. If you don't have family or friends who understand, or if you need more help, speak with your veterinarian or humane association and ask for a referral to pet grief support groups or veterinary bereavement counselors in your area. Several veterinary colleges around the country run hot lines, staffed by students, to offer a sympathetic ear and to help mourners vocalize their feelings about their pets. Check with your church or hospital for grief counseling. Calling a hot line is also a good way to cope. Remember, your grief is genuine and deserving of support.

CONSISTENCY

Maintain structure in your life by continuing to do the activities you did before the loss, with the exception of those you did with or for your pet. Do not allow this major disruption to snowball into every aspect of your life. Consistency will help you regain your bearings.

EDUCATION

Go to your local library. Ask the librarian to help you find books on the topic of your loss. Check the Bibliography on page 143 for additional books to guide you through your grief.

MEMORIALS

Perform a ritual when you feel the time is right. Some have funerals at a pet cemetery or memorials with friends and family. If your pet is cremated, have a special ceremony to sprinkle some of the ashes or have a special container for the ashes that honors the memory of your pet. If your pet is buried in a pet cemetery, have a small service with friends and family. Allowing and encouraging your family to have a funeral for the pet can be helpful. It provides a time to acknowledge the loss, share memories of the pet, and create a forum for the family to openly express emotions. While some friends or even family members may think having a funeral for your pet is foolish, don't let them take this special time away from you. Others may create a small shrine for a brief time. Have a candle-lighting ceremony with your family, friends, or by yourself. Read or write a poem to honor the special memory of your pet. Look at photos. Draw a picture to help you remember the joy your pet brought you. Create a memory book about your pet. Design a ritual that best meets your needs as you gather to pay tribute to your pet that was and always will be loved. Rituals can be helpful. Memorializing your pet makes the loss real and helps with healing. It allows the bereaved to express their feelings, pay tribute, and reflect. But, remember—do whatever feels right for YOU.

FEELINGS

Allow yourself to feel sadness and loss. Grief is a normal response to a normal occurrence, yet each person experiences it differently. Learn all you can about the grief process. It helps you realize that what you are experiencing is normal. The most important step you can take is to be honest about your feelings. Don't deny your pain, or your feelings of anger and guilt. Only by examining and coming to terms with your feelings can you begin to work through them. You have a right to feel pain and grief. Your pet, your best friend, your companion, has died, and you feel alone and bereaved. You have a right to feel anger and guilt, as well. Acknowledge your feelings first, then ask yourself whether the circumstances actually justify them. Don't be surprised or feel guilty if you can't or haven't cried. Feelings are natural and will take their own course.

Accept the feelings that come with grief. Pushing grief away doesn't make it go away. Express it. Cry, scream, kick the wall, pound the floor, talk it out. Do what helps you the most. If someone asks how you feel, try to be honest and express yourself. Don't say, "I'm fine" if you're not fine. Don't try to avoid grief by not thinking about your pet. Instead, reminisce about the good times. This will help you understand what your pet's loss actually means to you.

COUNSELING

If your grief is beginning to affect your functioning, get counseling. If you feel as though you cannot recover, or if you have thoughts of inflicting harm to yourself, contact a mental health professional immediately. If your grief continues intensely over a long period of time and you find yourself withdrawing from people, this could be a reflection of your inability to deal with loss and overcome it. Usually this is a sign that you may be dealing with other losses, or that you have unresolved grief issues, perhaps over a mother who died when you were young. You need to talk to someone who will be able to take that loss seriously.

It is fairly easy to find a counselor but it is important to choose a counselor based on criteria valued by you. Before committing to a session with a counselor, ask if you can have 10 or 15 minutes of his or her time to discuss some important issues with them to determine if working together is right for both of you. If you are at a difficult time in your grief work, perhaps a close friend or family member can handle this screening process for you. The following are some things to look for in a grief counselor when your pet has died.

- accepts or shares your values about animals
- accepts your spiritual beliefs
- accepts any healing activities you may engage in
- has experience with grief

Many universities have programs that help pet owners deal with the loss of their loved ones—from house pets to farm animals. Counselors, including veterinary students, offer advice on euthanasia decisions or emotional support. By calling these hotlines, the bereaved pet owners find someone who is sympathetic to their loss and understands what they are going through. They find someone who will listen to their story.

Call your local animal shelter for a referral. Many offer support groups and the facilitators of these groups often offer private counseling. You may also call your local hospice. They will know grief counselors in your community. See the Sources of Support on page 127 for Web sites related to grief counselors.

JOURNALING

Journal writing is a great way to keep in touch with yourself. As Oliver Wendell Holmes said, "What lies behind us and what lies before us are tiny matters, compared to what lies within us." One of the best ways to discover "what lies within" is to record thoughts, feelings, and aspirations in a journal. You may not feel like writing while you are grieving, but it is the best time to express yourself. That is when you need to write the most. If you write during your dark moods, you will find yourself feeling better as time goes by. Part of the reason to keep a journal is so that you get those horrible, painful parts of yourself out of your system so they don't fester inside of you. Read it over once a month to see how things are changing for you.

Some other ideas are: write to a pen pal and tell them everything about your pet, help someone who has a need, call an old friend and meet them for lunch or dinner. Rent a funny movie. Laughter is the best medicine! Indulge yourself in small pleasures. Remember that grief takes time. The questions and concerns you have right now may take some time to get answered. Be patient.

I'm Still Here

Friend, please don't mourn for me.
I'm still here, though you don't see.
I'm right by your side each night and day
And within your heart I long to stay.
My body is gone but I'm always near.
I'm everything you feel, see or hear.
My spirit is free, but I'll never depart
As long as you keep me alive in your heart.
I'll never wander out of your sight.
I'm the brightest star on a summer night.
I'll never be beyond your reach.
I'm the warm moist sand when you're at the beach.
I'm the colorful leaves when fall comes around

And the pure white snow that blankets the ground.
I'm the beautiful flowers of which you're so fond,
The clear cool water in a quiet pond.
I'm the first bright blossom you'll see in the spring
And the first warm raindrop that April will bring.
I'm the first ray of light when the sun starts to shine
And you'll see that the face in the moon is mine.
When you start thinking there's no one to love you,
You can talk to me through the Lord above you.
I'll whisper my answer through the leaves on the trees,
And you'll feel my presence in the soft summer breeze.
I'm the hot salty tears that flow when you weep
And the beautiful dreams that come while you sleep.
I'm the smile you see on a baby's face.
Just look for me, friend, I'm everyplace!

—*Author Unknown*

A Tribute to Our Best Friend
May 2003

I know you never met our canine friend, but he would have captured your heart with the shake of his paw. He thought everyone who came to our house came to visit him. His name was Ruger, and he entered into our lives twelve years ago, and has been part of our family ever since. Although he was a German Shepherd weighing close to 100 pounds, he was kind and gentle. He was always attuned to our emotions, and played a different role in each of our lives. If you were sad he was there to comfort you, and when you were happy he joined the fun.

This past week we had to make a heart wrenching decision to put our best friend to sleep. We had taken him to his veterinarian, because we thought he had an infection. We were told he had cancer that was growing aggressively, and it was time to let go, and let him be at peace. Therefore, our protector, confidante, and best friend died peacefully that day, taking a little piece of us with him.

I know it will get better in time, but oh how I wish I could fast-forward this pain. He taught us the true meaning of unconditional love, and left his paw print on our hearts. We brought him home, but not how we wanted it to be. He now rests in the backyard he loved so much, close to us. Your job is done now Ruger, you can rest peacefully.

—*With all our love, gone, but never forgotten,*
Dad, Mom, Charity, Brianne, Alyssa, and Brenden

CHAPTER 8
Helping the Bereaved Pet Owner

> We cannot banish dangers, but we can banish fears. We must not demean life by standing in awe of death.
> —*David Sarnoff*

Humans can be deeply affected by the loss of a pet. When the pet dies it can mark the loss of an intense relationship. Anyone who has ever loved a pet knows how deep that love can be. The loss that we feel after a pet dies is not widely recognized. The grief is often neglected and minimized because it isn't a real "human being." However, we need to realize that loss of a pet is loss of a family member and grief is a natural component of any loss. Pets offer us unconditional love, companionship, and protection. We establish relationships with our pets to meet a whole range of needs in our life. Working through grief requires a focused process. For individuals who are supportive of the bereaved pet owner, the following are a few tips for you to provide comfort during the grieving process:

- Know what to expect through the grieving process. Typical reactions to grief include the same reactions you would feel with a loss of any friend or family member. If the death of the pet is unexpected, these feelings are intensified.
- Be patient and understanding with the grieving pet owner. Although you may not have a special attachment with an animal, your friend or relative does and these feelings should be respected.
- Allow and encourage the pet owner to express the emotions involved in the pain, sorrow, and loss of the pet. Allow the person to cry. It

is not healthy to stifle emotions. Talk about the relationship with the dead pet—including feelings of love, guilt, and anger.
- Encourage the owner to focus on the positive aspects of the relationship with the pet. Reminiscing about pleasant memories the person had with the pet will help them work through their grief. Pushing or denying those feelings can only cause pain later.
- Help to organize a flexible, limited schedule of activities through available and suitable family, relatives, or friends.
- Do not try to push the grieving pet owner too fast, as it may discourage facing the reality of the loss.
- Offer assistance where needed. Run errands or do household chores when the person is having a really bad day. The grieving person may have other pets that need to be walked or cared for. Offer to pet sit so they can take some time off to be alone if this is something that might be needed.
- Watch for signs of complicated grief, such as insomnia, loss of appetite, lack of involvement in activities, etc. and, if necessary, suggest counseling.
- Above all, *actively* listen to what the person has to say. Be present!
- What about PTO (personal time off)—allowing employees to use sick leave or vacation time to allow the grieving process to regain some semblance of order or balance? I am not proposing bereavement leave, and there are some problems with a sick leave policy which allows for caring for a sick animal, but there should be allowances made under these conditions—such as using sick time, personal time, or vacation. Some companies already allow employees a day or more off in these circumstances, but they're in the minority. It would be nice if more businesses made time available, especially for grieving over the loss of one's beloved pet.

If bereavement counseling is necessary, usually one or two sessions is all that is necessary. Pet owners often need validation—with counselors informing clients that grief is a natural and individualized response to a loss of a pet. This helps to normalize the experience. Letting clients know there is no right or wrong way to grieve gives them permission to express their loss in culturally and personally relevant ways. Professional counselors can help pet owners work through their grief by encouraging them to write or talk about their thoughts and feelings just as they do with clients who have experienced the loss of a human friend. Many pet owners are not aware of their attachment to their pets or how large a role the pet played in their lives. Counselors can also help clients explore anger, blame, and guilt. They can assist them in finding support systems. There are many support groups that provide education and informational resources on the interrelationship of humans, animals, and the environment. These groups maintain a directory of pet loss resources that includes pet loss counselors and hotlines. Check page 127 for a list of support services.

The Creation

When God had made the earth and sky, the flowers and the trees,
He then made all the animals, the fish, the birds and bees.
And when at last He'd finished, not one was quite the same.
He said, "I'll walk this world of mine and give each one a name."
And so He traveled far and wide and everywhere He went,
A little creature followed Him until its' strength was spent.
When all were named upon the earth and in the sky and sea,
The little creature said, "Dear Lord, there's not one left for me."
Kindly the Father said to him, "I've left you to the end.
I've turned my own name back to front and called you dog,
   my friend."

—Author Unknown

BUDDY

"Buddy . . . Buddy, stop it . . . Bud Robert!" How many times over the last 12 years did we say those words—garbage cans turned over, new shoes destroyed, food destroyed, food stolen right off our plates! Buddy was a 65-pound, tri-colored basset hound whom we adored.

In June 2001 I admitted my husband to the hospital for major back surgery. The next day I saw Buddy collapse in the backyard. My mom and I rushed him to the veterinarian. After being admitted, we learned his liver was not functioning properly due to congestive heart failure. I spent each morning with Buddy in a sterile, cold room praying, begging, and bargaining with God not to take his life, and I spent the rest of the day at the hospital with my husband reassuring me Buddy was a fighter.

Buddy gave it everything he had, but he died the day before I brought my husband home from the hospital. As I helped my husband up the sidewalk with his walker, he started crying, and I thought he was in pain. He said it was the first time in 12 years he didn't hear Buddy bark when we came home. So, we stood outside our front door and cried.

Over the next several weeks, we cried and hugged each other a lot. The house was too quiet. We didn't hear Buddy's feet tapping on the ceramic tile or see the white tip of his tail coming around the corner. We were miserable. Buddy was more than just our pet—he was our boy, the joy of our home. He was gone, and we didn't know where to find him.

Our family and friends kept reassuring us Buddy had a wonderful life. But our hearts were broken. How do you heal a broken heart? Six weeks later when I saw my husband holding Buddy's picture and sobbing, I knew what I had to do.

A few days later I walked in the house and placed a 14-pound "bundle of trouble" named Annie in my husband's arms. And that is where this beautiful tri-colored basset still sleeps today after five months and 24 more pounds. Every day Annie reminds us of Buddy—stubborn, curious, and messy. Annie would have loved her big brother. I know we always will. We still cry over Buddy, but now we can smile, too—we are beginning to heal.

—Colleen Miller, personal communication

CHAPTER 9
Dealing with Guilt

> All of the animals except man know that the principal business of life is to enjoy it.
> —*Samuel Butler*

Guilt is a word that can invoke in us the deepest and most terrible feelings of loss. It is a normal response to failing some duty or obligation. It differs from disappointment in that guilt admits to failing to perform at a level well within our competence. It is closely related to the emotion of shame, which is based on a negative response that could have been prevented. We say things like, "I should have done more," or "Did I put her down too soon?" We beat ourselves up for so many "if-onlys." Why do we do this to ourselves? We do it because we loved our pets. We do it because we wish we could have done more, or wish we had not done what we did. No matter what we say we cannot bring them back. We cannot change what we did or did not do. It may be difficult, but it is important to admit that you are human and forgive yourself for not being perfect. Promising to do things differently the next time and then achieving this goal will help you feel better.

We are sensitive human beings with faults. We don't know everything. The mistakes we make, we make with the best of intentions. To hurt ourselves with the terrible additional pain of guilt is to do disservice to the love we felt for our beloved pet. You did the best you knew how to do at the time. Even if you feel that you didn't do what you should have or could have done, you learned from the experience. Now, you need to stop hurting yourself. Don't torture yourself with accusations and guilt. You did what you thought was right at the time and you did it with the intention of love.

Your loving pet has died and is out of pain, but you still torture yourself with the pain of guilt and doubt. True, it is human to do this, but are you being fair to yourself? Think about this. You are basically a good person, so recognize the good qualities you have. Stop inflicting pain on yourself for what you could or should have done. You loved deeply. You have a deep capacity for love that many do not. Be proud of that! You took a beautiful creature and gave it everything you could. You petted it, walked it, fed it, and changed the litter box time and time again. You played and stroked your pet. You were sleepless on the nights your pet was ill. You cared for your pet and did everything you knew to do at the time. And, when you looked in its eyes, you knew your pet understood the love you have for one another.

Unfortunately, there is usually no place for death in our comfort zone. It scares and mystifies us, so we politely avoid thinking about it whenever we can. When death does come, the shock easily can be distorted into an intense feeling of personal inadequacy and guilt. Our emotions tell us we have failed to perform as well as we should have. It makes us feel as if we are responsible for letting our pet die. Your life and energy are being wasted feeling guilt because you wish things had been different. This is misplaced and negative energy. Remember, guilt is a normal, personal, human response to having committed some perceived offense. We are human and we make mistakes. Don't we deserve forgiveness and some compassion as well? Forgive yourself!

Responsibility now must be to one's self. Be the wonderful person that your pet saw in you! You will move through grief in your own unique way and time frame. Preserve the wonderful memories you have of your pet! Reach out to others who are suffering over the death of their pet. Use your pain to make things better for other pets, and for the animals out there that are alone and lost. There are so many people out there who need you. Volunteer your time at a local pet hospital, pet cemetery, or Humane Society.

CHAPTER 10

Do Pets Grieve?

Death . . . the last sleep? No, the final awakening.
—*Walter Scott*

The death of a loved one can be a difficult and painful experience. It can be just as hard on a pet that is suffering the loss of an owner or another pet within the home. Pets observe every change in a household, and are bound to notice the absence of a companion. Many people find it hard to believe that animals can form very firm attachments with each other. Animals that live together often bond together and certainly notice when another animal is missing from the household. Bonded pairs often show strong attachment to one another and often the surviving animal grieves for its companion. Cats grieve for dogs, and dogs for cats. Like humans, animals can experience feelings of grief and depression in times of loss. Even pets that outwardly seem to barely get along will exhibit intense stress reactions when separated. In fact, grieving pets can show many reactions identical to those experienced by the bereaved pet owner. The surviving pet(s) may become restless, anxious, and depressed. There may also be much sighing, excessive vocalization, inactivity, and sleep and eating disturbances. The animal may frequent places that the other pet stayed, such as favorite sleeping spots or places that they played together. Often, grieving pets will search for their dead companions and crave more attention from their owners.

A question often asked is, "Should I let the surviving animals see and smell their dead companion?" There is no evidence that doing so will help the surviving pet(s), but some people claim that it does. Usually, all it accomplishes is to make the owner feel better. Therefore, if the owner wants have the surviving pets "say goodbye," then it should be allowed.

It may take some time for the animal to get over the loss. Make sure you don't accidentally reinforce negative behavior by trying to give the pet more attention. If it's not eating its regular food, don't keep changing the food. Don't try to give it favorite little food treats. All that does is create a more finicky pet. Your pet may learn that it can get more attention and more tasty food treats if it acts this way. You want to give a lot of extra attention to other surviving pet(s)—not with food but with love. It is important to keep the pet's routine as normal as possible. Maintain consistency in exercise, feeding schedule, and amount of attention. This will help both you and your surviving pets. Be sure to stay with them as they may also wander away looking for the missing animal. It may take some time for surviving pets to stop waiting for the companion to return.

Remember, too, if you are going to introduce a new pet, your surviving pet(s) may not accept the newcomer right away, but new bonds will grow in time. Allow the surviving animals to work out the new dominance hierarchy themselves. There may be some scuffles and fights as the animals work out the new pecking order but, in time, they will learn to accept one another. Talk to your veterinarian about how to do this. Meanwhile, the love of your surviving pets can be wonderfully healing for your own grief.

GOOD BYE OLD FRIEND:
A LOVING TRIBUTE TO A SPECIAL DOG

The old dog lay quietly on the soft, white blanket looking up with trusting eyes at his master of 13 years. The once proud and strong Dalmatian was now feeble and mostly deaf. The limbs that once trotted powerfully up the driveway to guide arriving cars to the house, now shook uncontrollably. The intelligent and gentle eyes that looked out from the sleek head were now mostly filled with confusion and great pain.

The old dog's master and friend held up the syringe filled with the clear, pink solution and looked at his long-time companion. "I'm going to miss you old friend," he whispered. He placed a hand on top of the broad soft head and gently stroked the great dog's velvet ears. The tail thumped weakly in response. Then with a precision that comes with long years of experience, he inserted the needle expertly into the old dog's vein and slowly depressed the plunger. A sob caught in his throat as he watched his friend crumple into the folds of the blanket. He sat and watched the chest rise and fall as he murmured gently to the dying dog. As his old protector and companion took his last breath, he placed his stethoscope to the now silent chest and listened for a moment. Then he folded a portion of the blanket over the lifeless body.

He let the other dogs in so that they might understand the new status of the household. No one knows what a dog really thinks and feels, but he felt that doing this was important. Two of the dogs ran around as if nothing new had transpired. But the smallest of them all, the one that had grown up with the old Dalmatian, lay down quietly next to the inert body and rested his tiny muzzle on the great dog's paw.

Silently he dug a grave in the wet ground, his tears mingling freely with the rain. He had picked this final resting spot carefully, placing it between two other old friends, a beloved dog and cat that the old Dalmatian had spent many happy years with.

It had not been an easy decision. He had counseled and empathized with many of his clients who had wrestled with the same choice. He himself had agonized over it for a long time. But he finally knew that he needed to help his friend escape the constant pain that all of his veterinary training and years of experience could not erase.

As the last shovel of dirt was placed over the grave, he felt deeply saddened that he'd never again gaze upon the soft, wise eyes, but knew in his heart that his old friend was finally at peace.

—*Author Unknown*

CHAPTER 11
Final Farewells

A righteous man regardeth the life of his beasts.
—*Proverbs xii, 10*

When the family pet dies, you must choose how to handle the remains. Sometimes, in the midst of grief, it may seem easiest to leave the pet at the clinic for disposal. Find out what this means if you want to know. Some clients are horrified when they find out their pet was taken to a landfill. Check with your veterinarian to find out whether there is a fee for such disposal. Some shelters also accept remains, though many charge a fee. Some owners cannot regard their beloved pet as only the corpse of an animal. Millions of people have close attachments to their pets or to animals they have worked with: the horse who pulled the milkman's wagon, the dog who guided its visually impaired owner, or the circus trainer's elephant. Attachment does not automatically end at death, whether the loss is that of another human or of an animal companion.

If you prefer a more formal option, several are available. Home burial is a popular choice, if you have sufficient property for it. It is economical and enables you to design your own funeral ceremony at little cost. However, city regulations usually prohibit pet burials, and this is not a good choice for renters or people who move frequently.

The pet cemetery is another example of the way in which some people attempt to cope with the death of an animal companion. To many, a pet cemetery provides a sense of dignity and permanence. Owners appreciate the serene surroundings and care of the gravesite. Many are spacious, with safeguards against the land being used for other purposes and with funding to provide future grounds keeping. Cemetery costs vary depending on the services you select, as well as upon the type of pet you have. A general rule of thumb is that pet burial costs 10 percent of what it may cost to bury a human. The International Association of Pet Cemeteries' (IAPC) voluntary standards state that a good pet cemetery should consist of at least five acres, possess an endowed care fund, be well maintained, and be restricted by a deed of trust. The IAPC is an organization that attempts to set professional standards and provide public information.

The modern version of the pet cemetery is believed to have started in France around the turn of the 20th century. In addition to dogs and cats, horses, monkeys, rabbits, and birds have been buried at Le Cimetriere des Chiens, located on the tiny Island of the Ragpickers in the Seine. The most famous animal buried there is Rin-Tin-Tin. The impulse to honor the memory of an animal companion through a funeral and burial process has been expressed throughout history. There are 145 pet cemeteries in the United States that are presently affiliated with the IAPC. Pet cemeteries have invited parody and mockery on occasion. People have sometimes behaved oddly after the death of a four-footed or feathered friend. Nevertheless, those who understand and value the bonds of affection that can form between humans and animals may judge that showing "too much" love is not the worst thing that might be said of a person.

Cremation is a less expensive option that allows you to handle your pet's remains in a variety of ways. You can bury them, scatter them in a favorite location, place them in a columbarium, or even keep them with you in a decorative urn. There are a wide variety of urns available— at a wide variety of prices. Check with your veterinarian, pet shop, or telephone directory for options available in your state. Consider your living situation, personal values, religious practices, finances, and future plans when making your decision. It is also wise to make such plans in advance, rather than hurriedly in the midst of grief.

Some owners arrange to donate their pet's remains to a nearby veterinary school in the same way that people donate their bodies to medical science. A few arrange for taxidermy, although the results are often disappointing. Taxidermy is a technique for preserving animals and showing them as they looked when alive. The word taxidermy comes from two Greek words meaning "arrangement" and "skin." Museums of natural history exhibit birds, fish, squirrels, antelopes, tigers, and other wild animals in their natural settings.

In ancient times, those who believed in the promise of another tomorrow mummified their pets at their natural passing. These pets were mummified so they could continue on to their next life. People of long ago realized that there is a quality about some animals that makes them human and divine. These fortunate animals of ancient aristocrats were treasured during their lives and at their natural passing. Royal mummification arrangements were made for them. Once again, in Salt Lake City, there are licensed, certified thanatogeneticists who will immediately begin the mummification process on your pet. After being wrapped in fine linens and bathed with fragrant herbs, oils, and resins, your pet will be placed within a bronze mummiform and rejoined with you. Mummification supposedly shelters the essence and body of your pet forever and through this singular form of permanent body preservation, you pet will enter eternity in all of his splendor and beauty.

Text Taken from a Memorial

. . . For if the dog be well remembered, if sometimes she leaps through your dreams actual as in life, eyes kindling, laughing, begging, it matters not where that dog sleeps. On a hill where the wind is unrebuked and the trees are roaring, or beside a stream she knew in puppyhood, or somewhere in the flatness of a pastureland where most exhilarating cattle graze. It is one to a dog, and all one to you, and nothing is gained and nothing lost—if memory lives. But there is one best place to bury a dog.

If you bury her in this spot, she will come to you when you call—come to you over the grim, dim frontiers of death, and down the well-remember path and to your side again. And though you may call a dozen living dogs to heel, they shall not growl at her nor resent her coming, for she belongs there.

People may scoff at you, who see no lightest blade of grass bent by her footfall, who hear no whimper, people who have never really had a dog. Smile at them, for your shall know something that is hidden from them.

The one best place to bury a good dog is in the heart of her master . . .

—Anonymous

BOATSWAIN

After the death of "Boatswain," the Newfoundland who was the trusted friend of Lord Byron, the famed English poet has a monument erected on his grave at Newstead Abbey. Then he wrote the following poem, which was etched on one side of the octagonal shaft:

When some proud son of man returns to earth
Unknown to glory, but upheld by birth,
The sculptor's art exhausts the pomp of woe,
And storied urns record who rests below.
When all is done, upon the tomb is seen,
Not what he was, but what he should have been.
But the poor dog, in life the firmest friend,
The first to welcome, the foremost to defend,
Whose honest heart is still his master's own,
Who labors, lives, fights, breathes for him alone,
Unhonored falls, unnoticed all his worth,
Denied in heaven the soul he held on earth.
While man, vain insect, hopes to be forgiven,
And claims himself a sole, exclusive heaven.
Ye! Who behold, perchance, this simple urn,
Pass on; it honours none you wish to mourn.
To mark a friend's remains these stones rise,
I have never known but one—and here he lies.
—*Lord Byron*

If you can start the day without caffeine . . .
If you can always be cheerful, ignoring aches and pains . . .
If you can resist complaining and boring people with your troubles . . .
If you can eat the same food every day and be grateful for it . . .
If you can understand when your loved ones are too busy to give you any time . . .
If you can overlook it when those you love take it out on you, when through no fault of your own, something goes wrong . . .
If you can take criticism and blame without resentment . . .
If you can ignore a friend's limited education and never correct him . . .
If you can face the world without lies and deceit . . .
If you can conquer tension without medical help . . .
If you can sleep without the aid of drugs . . .
If you can say honestly that deep in your heart you have no prejudice against creed, color, religion, or politics . . .
If you can give love unconditionally without pressure or expectations . . .
Then my friend . . .
You are almost as good as your DOG.

CHAPTER 12
Pets and Spirituality

> Parting is all we know of heaven and all we need of hell.
> —*Emily Dickinson*

Have you given any thought to what you believe about reincarnation? Will your pet rise again? "Yes," some faiths say. The Eastern belief is that animals have souls. Western views are more complicated. There are those that question whether animals have souls. Across time and cultures, many religions have taught that animals are at least partially souled. The word *animal* derives from the Latin *anima*, meaning "soul." Still, the issue has been subject to many contradictions. Jainism, Buddhism, and Hinduism teach that animal souls, or essences, are equal to those of humans. Much of Christianity, meanwhile, reserves the immortal soul for humans. Aristotle set the pattern for Western thought. He maintained that both man and animals had souls but that animals were sentient beings whose mortal souls consisted of instinctual sensations. Humans were rational beings with immortal souls. In the Middle Ages, St. Thomas Aquinas concurred with Aristotle and spun Christian thinking in a direction that continues to this day. The belief was furthered by 17th century philosopher Rene Descartes, who said animals were merely well-oiled machines without thoughts, feelings, or immortal souls. St. Francis of Assisi, the Catholic saint known for his love of animals, believed that animal souls were immortal. Some churches even hold ceremonies, known as "blessing of the animals," in honor of St. Francis. John Wesley, who founded Methodism, spoke of the eternal souls of animals.

Most pet owners don't really seem to care much what religions say, but some people are very affected when their religion claims that pets don't have souls. They prefer the hopeful belief that they'll see their special friends again someday. Some comments are, "If my cats and dogs aren't there to meet me, then I don't want to go there either," or "If my babies aren't allowed in heaven, then forget about me!" ABC News took a poll and found that 47 percent of all pet owners said their furry and feathered friends go to heaven. Thirty-five percent said pets do not spend life in eternity and 18 percent have no opinion. Of those who do not have pets, 38 percent believe pets go on to a better place after death, 48 percent think that it's total nonsense, and 14 percent have no opinion (Reverend Vance Rains, a pastor at The United Methodist Church in Port St. Lucie; *The News*, Saturday, October 6, 2001).

According to animal communicators, humans have the ability to communicate telepathically with all species. Of course, this does require the proper mindset and training. Communicating with an animal is a two-way process—sending and receiving. Telepathy can be done in person or at a distance. A good example of this is when you are thinking of someone and they call! Is this a coincidence or mental telepathy? Animal communicators say that being able to talk to an animal is not a gift possessed by a few special people—everyone is born with the ability to do this. This ability appeared more commonly in ancient cultures. If you love animals, then you are already doing animal communication on some level. It takes a desire to study and practice to become good at it.

In *Animal Death, A Spiritual Journey*, Penelope Smith, an Animal Communication Specialist, says she communicates with animals telepathically, both living and dead, and counsels owners to assist them toward a more ideal relationship with their animals. She also performs grief counseling for those whose animals have left the earth. For some of you, this may seem a bit farfetched, but if you are harboring a lot of grief inside you and are desperate for relief, you may find you are open to things you never before considered. In Smith's book, *Animals, Our Return to Wholeness*, she encourages pet owners to make contact with their departed friends. These communications appear to be uplifting experiences for the bereaved. To make contact with your beloved pet, sit in a quiet place and visualize your animal. See them as they were in life. Tell them you would like to feel them—to communicate with them. Let them know you are hurting and that you want to be touched. You may not feel them right away. There are a lot of ways to be contacted. You may be doing the laundry or washing dishes and you'll know they are right beside you. You may hear them scratch at the door or run through the house. If you invite them, they will make their presence felt. Often they visit in dreams, as do living animals, because we are most accessible during those times. When you awake, trust what you get and ask what you are supposed to learn from it.

Life continues, energy patterns simply change and, because of this change, we are not as likely to be aware of the pattern that has evolved. Do not be surprised if you feel your pet around, hear sounds that make you think your pet is in the house, or even see your pet. No, you are not crazy—you are experiencing a magical touch or bond that simply links you to another reality—if only for an instant.

On September 8th, National Pet Memorial Day, believers in pet afterlife come together at pet cemeteries all over to celebrate the souls of their beloved pets. These pet owners truly believe they will meet their friends again in the afterlife. Much of the belief in pet heaven comes from people whose only companionship is provided by their pets. Pets bring great joy into the lives of many people. They become members of the family. They are a great source of enjoyment, companionship, protection, and love. When a pet dies, it is quite normal to grieve for them and to miss their presence. It is also quite normal to hope that they will be seen again some day. Humans have a tendency to translate what makes them happy in this life into the spirit world. So what? If it gives them faith, then so be it!

No one knows for sure what happens after death. We don't know what heaven is like, but if we believe that what God has planned for us includes all things that we love, it makes living life a lot easier while we are here on earth.

A Bridge Called Love

It takes us back to brighter years, to happier sunlit days.
And to precious moments that will be with us always.
And these fond recollections are treasured in the heart
To bring us always close to those from whom we had to part.
There is a bridge of memories from earth to Heaven above.
It keeps our dear ones near us.
It's the bridge that we call love.
—*Author Unknown*

A Little Dog Angel

High up in the courts of heaven today a little dog angel waits;
With the other angels he will not play, but he sits alone at
    the gates.
"For I know my master will come," says he, "and when he comes he
    will call for me."
The other angels pass him by as they hurry toward the throne,
And he watches them with a wistful eye as he sits at the gates alone.

But I know if I just wait patiently that someday my master will call
  for me."
And his master, down on earth below, as he sits in his easy chair,
Forgets sometimes, and whispers low to the dog who is not there.
And the little dog angel cocks his ears and dreams that his maser's
  voice he hears.
And when at last his master waits outside in the dark and cold,
For the hand of death to open the door, that leads to those courts
  of gold,
He will hear a sound through the gathering dark, a little dog
  angel's bark.

—*Author Unknown*

Poem For Cats

And God asked the feline spirit, Are you ready to come home?
Oh, yes, quite so, replied the precious soul,
And, as a cat, you know I am most able to decide anything for myself.
Are you coming then? asked God. Soon, replied the whiskered angel,
But I must come slowly for my human friends are troubled.
For you see, they need me, quite certainly.
But don't they understand? asked God, that you'll never leave them?
That your souls are intertwined for all eternity? That nothing is
  created or destroyed?
It just is . . . forever and ever and ever.
Eventually they will understand, replied the glorious cat.
For I will whisper into their hearts that I am always with them.
I just am—forever and ever and ever.

—*Author Unknown*

Dogs in Heaven?

An old man and his dog were walking down this dirt road with fences on both sides. They came to a gate in the fence and looked in. It was a nice grassy, woody area—just what a huntin' dog and man would like. But, it had a sign saying "No Trespassing" so they walked on. They came to a beautiful gate with a person in white robes standing there. "Welcome to Heaven" he said. The old man was happy and started in with his dog following him. The gatekeeper stopped him. "Dogs aren't allowed. I'm sorry but he can't come with you."

"What kind of Heaven won't allow dogs? If he can't come in, then I will stay out with him. He's been my faithful companion all his life. I can't desert him now."

"Suit yourself, but I have to warn you. The Devil's on this road and he'll try to sweet talk you into his area. He'll promise you anything, but the dog can't go there either. If you won't leave the dog, you'll spend Eternity on this road."

So the old man and dog went on. They came to a rundown fence with a gap in it, no gate—just a hole. Another old man was inside. "S'cuse me, Sir. My dog and I are getting mighty tired; mind if we come in and sit in the shade for awhile?"

"Of course, I don't mind. There's some cold water under that tree over there. Make yourselves comfortable."

"You're sure my dog can come in? The man down the road said dogs weren't allowed anywhere."

"Would you come in if you had to leave the dog?"

"No sir. That's why I didn't go to Heaven. He said the dog couldn't come in. We'll be spending Eternity on this road, and a glass of cold water and some shade would be mighty fine right about now. But, I won't come in if my buddy here can't come, too, and that's final."

The man smiled a big smile and said "Welcome to Heaven."

"You mean this is Heaven? Dogs ARE allowed? How come that fellow down the road said they weren't?"

"That was the Devil and he gets all the people who are willing to give up a life-long companion for a comfortable place to stay. They soon find out their mistake, but then it's too late. The dogs come here, the fickle people stay there. GOD wouldn't allow dogs to be banned from Heaven. After all, HE created them to be man's companions in life. Why would he separate them in death?"

—Author Unknown

CHAPTER 13

Getting Another Pet

> A friend is a present you give yourself.
> —*Robert Louis Stevenson*

Should I get a new pet right away? Generally, the answer is no. One needs time to work through grief and loss before attempting to build a rapport with a new pet. If your emotions are still in turmoil, you may resent a new pet for trying to "make you forget" or "take the place" of the other pet. It is not helpful to ignore the importance of the loss or to be embarrassed by it. Also, potentially damaging is attempting to deny the importance of the pet by quickly acquiring a replacement pet. Instead, allow the death of a pet to be one of those lessons in life that help us to learn about grief.

If your pet was euthanized as the result of an infectious illness, then your veterinarian may advise you to let a period of time elapse before getting another animal. This is mainly to reduce the risk of infection that may still be in your home. Aside from this, it is a personal decision. Some people cannot live without animal companionship and need to get another pet immediately. Others may consider this to be disloyal or disrespectful to their former companion. Some need a period of time to come to terms with the loss of their pet—how long this takes will vary from person to person.

Introducing a pet into families that face the threat of the loss of a parent or child can, in many cases, prove to be a valuable measure of mental therapy. The pet gives the caregivers a living companion that will not usually be a competitor for the surviving parent's affection. Even more important, it gives the only child something to play with and occupy its time when everyone in the family is preoccupied with the dying loved one. When the parent or sibling dies, the pet plays a crucial role by providing the child with a sympathetic, nonjudgmental listener. With the pet, the child can become immersed in his grief and speak repeatedly about the beloved parent, or evaluate his own guilt in bringing about the death without being judged.

Whatever your decision is, remember the new pet will not replace the one that has died. Don't expect your pet to be "just like" the one that died. Your new pet will have a personality all his own. Avoid getting a "look alike" pet, which makes comparisons all the more likely. It is good advice not to give a new pet the same name or nickname as the former one. Try hard not to compare the new pet to the old one. It will only make loving this pet more difficult in the long run.

My Cat

Close by a wall
Whose bricks were all
Rainsoaked and old
A little cat
Hunched where he sat
Shivering and cold.
Deaf to his cry
Crowds hurried by
Past his meow.
I couldn't bear
To see him there.
He's my cat now.
We have long talks
Lincoln Park walks
Cream puffs and pie.
A windowpane
Shuts out the rain
Keeps my cat dry.
—*Author Unknown*

To Love Again

Oh what unhappy twist of fate has brought you homeless to my gate,
The gate where once another stood to beg for shelter, warmth, and food?
For from that day I ceased to be the master of my destiny,

While she, with purr and velvet paw became within my house
   the law.
She scratched the furniture and shed and claimed the middle of
   my bed.
She ruled in arrogance and pride and broke my heart the day
   she died.
So if you really think, oh cat, I'd willingly relive all that,
Because you come forlorn and thin, well don't just stand
   there—come on in!

—*Author Unknown*

In Memoriam . . . for my cat, Buddy, 1991-2002

Long ago, on a bright summer day,
I brought you into my home and my heart.
What a wondrous sight to watch you play;
Ever quick to leap and pounce and dart.

A tiny fluff of gray and white, my precious kitten boy.
The flick of your tail and baritone purrs: such pleasure!
For thousands of days to come, your love and trust were
   pure joy.
Our nightly snuggles . . . moments to treasure.

Too swiftly passed those happy years.
Slow of gait and growing frail, your sublime mystique
   deeper grew.
Long and loving good-byes were said with tears.
You soon would cross beyond, we both knew.

Not long ago, on a bright winter day,
The angels came while you were asleep.
At peace and so gently you passed away.
Through the prism of my tears, my Buddy
Will forever be a rainbow in my heart to keep.

One day we will together in Heaven be,
Once again, never to part, my Buddy and me.

—*Helen A. Jones, January 12, 2003*

CHAPTER 14
Animal Abuse

> Think occasionally of the suffering of which you spare yourself the sight.
> —*Albert Schweitzer*

Violent acts toward animals have long been recognized as indicators of a dangerous psychopathy that does not confine itself to animals. According to Robert K. Ressier, who developed profiles of serial killers for the Federal Bureau of Investigation, murderers very often start out by killing and torturing animals as kids. Studies have now convinced sociologists, lawmakers, and the courts that acts of cruelty toward animals deserve our attention. They can be the first sign of a violent pathology that may lead to serious harm or death to humans.

Animal abuse is not just the result of a personality flaw in the abuser—it's a symptom of a deep mental disturbance. Research shows that people who commit acts of cruelty against animals don't stop there—many of them move on to human beings. Some notorious killers in history include:

- Patrick Sherrill, who killed 14 coworkers at a post office and then shot himself, had a history of stealing local pets and allowing his own dog to attack and mutilate them.
- Earl Kenneth Shriner, who raped, stabbed, and mutilated a seven-year-old boy, had been widely known in his neighborhood as the man who put firecrackers in dogs' rectums and strung up cats.
- Brenda Spencer, who opened fire at a San Diego school, killing two children and injuring nine others, had repeatedly abused cats and dogs, often by setting their tails on fire.

- Albert DeSalvo, the "Boston Strangler" who killed 13 women, trapped dogs and cats in orange crates and shot arrows through the boxes in his youth.
- Carroll Edward Cole, executed for five of the 35 murders of which he was accused, said his first act of violence as a child was to strangle a puppy.
- Jeffrey Dahmer had impaled dogs' heads, frogs, and cats on sticks.

More recently, high school killers such as 15-year-old Kip Kinkel in Springfield, Oregon, and Luke Woodham, 16, in Pearl, Mississippi, tortured animals before embarking on shooting sprees. Columbine High School students Eric Harris and Dylan Kiebold, who shot and killed 12 classmates before turning their guns on themselves, bragged about mutilating animals to their friends.

According to Dr. Harold S. Koplewicz, director of the Child Study Center at New York University, there is a common pattern to all of the shootings in recent years: a child who has symptoms of aggression toward his peers, an interest in fire, cruelty to animals, social isolation, and many warning signs that the school has ignored. Many of these childhood violent acts went unexamined until they were directed toward humans. Margaret Mead said, "One of the most dangerous things that can happen to a child is to kill or torture an animal and get away with it."

Domestic abuse is usually directed toward weak individuals by those who thrive on power and control. Animal abuse and child abuse often go hand in hand with domestic abuse. Parents who neglect an animal's need for proper care or abuse animals may also be guilty of abusing their own children. While animal abuse is an important sign of child abuse, the parent isn't always the one harming the animal. Children who abuse animals may be repeating a lesson learned from their parents. They are reacting to anger or frustration through violence—directed at the family pet—the one thing they are able to control in their life. Occasionally, a pet is given to a child by a parent and is thus identified with that parent. If the parent later dies, the child may express his anger at the parent's "desertion" by attacking and even killing the pet. This is a frequent occurrence among emotionally disturbed children. It seems as though, by experimenting with death and by inflicting death on an inoffensive creature, the child imagines himself to be the master of life, the conqueror of death. At this critical time in a child's life, his needs for affection, support, companionship, and ego gratification are no longer being adequately met (Levinson, 1972).

Schools, parents, and courts that shrug off animal abuse as a minor crime are ignoring a time bomb ready to explode. Communities should be penalizing animal abusers, examining families for other signs of violence, and requiring intensive counseling for perpetrators. Society must recognize that abuse to any living creature is unacceptable and endangers everyone. Children should be taught to care for and respect animals in their own right. We need to promote a more positive and nurturing relationship between children and animals.

If you witness animal abuse or neglect, please contact your local Humane Society, animal shelter, or animal control agency immediately. In most areas, those agencies have both the jurisdiction and capability to investigate and resolve these situations. They rely on concerned citizens to be their eyes and ears in the community and to report animal suffering. You can choose to remain anonymous if you wish, although giving your name to your local humane agency will enable that agency to follow up with you when necessary. If you only *think* an animal is being abused, you should still contact the proper authorities in the town where the incident is occurring. Be sure you have the abuser's name and address and where the offense is taking place.

You can find the name and number of your local Humane Society or animal control agency by looking in the Yellow Pages of your telephone book under "Humane Society," or "animal control," or by calling Information. If there is no local animal shelter or animal control agency in your community, then report the incident to your local police department immediately. For your information, the Humane Society of the United States (HSUS) does not have animal control capabilities. They are not associated with animal control agencies in any way nor do they have direct control over any animal shelter. The HSUS is strictly a resource for these organizations by providing them with educational materials, training opportunities, and recommended operations guidelines. They do conduct large-scale, national investigations covering a number of animal issues.

HOW CAN YOU HELP?

Evaluate the Situation

Sometimes we misinterpret what appears to be neglect seen from a neighbor's yard. If you believe an animal is not being fed, or left for hours without water, or has no way to get out of inclement weather, look more closely during different times of the day to be sure this is not a single event. The water bowls may be under cover where you are unable to see them. Maybe the owner feeds the dog every morning before leaving for work—while you are still asleep—and then removes the bowl. Maybe the dog has a pet door into the garage or shed that is not visible to you. Maybe the dog prefers to be outside no matter what the weather, so you never see him go inside the pet door.

Report the Incident

If the animal is crying or barking, doesn't get fed or given water every day, and appears to need your help, do not hesitate to contact the proper authorities. Physical abuse is more immediately recognizable. Definite acts of abuse are choking, setting tails on fire, putting rubber bands around limbs or tails, dunking heads under water, and kicking or hitting repeatedly. Seeing this type of abuse might enrage you and make you want to confront the abuser. I wouldn't advise this move unless you are positive that a friendly, informal chat will make the person more caring toward his pet. Chances are this is not going to be the case. If you can safely take photographs or videotape the incident, do so. This evidence is invaluable to investigators.

When the Abuse Appears to be Caused by a Child

The parent may not be aware of this behavior. However, animal abuse and child abuse are closely linked so it would be better to let a humane officer investigate the situation. If there appears to be a possibility of neglect, the humane officer will investigate the situation. If you are concerned about being blamed for reporting the abuse or worried about any retaliation against you, tell the humane officer that you wish to remain anonymous. The humane officer will visit the home and determine the action needed to alleviate the animal's suffering. Oftentimes, neglect is caused by owners not understanding what their pet needs, so the officer spends 90 percent of the time educating people on how to correctly care for their pet. Some owners, however, do neglect their pets because they simply don't care. When confronted by a humane officer, these owners may decide to relinquish the animals rather than being bothered with properly caring for them in the future.

If the pet is seriously unhealthy or obviously being abused, the humane officer may remove the animal while the investigation is under way. You can help in several ways: alert the officer if the owner gets another pet and, if charges are brought against the owner, you can offer to testify or sign a complaint, since neglect is difficult to prove. In the case of violent abuse, witnesses are rare, so you may be the only person who can testify about the abuse. It is very important that you do not attempt to remove a pet from a potentially abusive or neglectful environment. Not only is this illegal, but it is also very dangerous! It is also not protecting future animals that the owner may get and abuse.

Learn About Local and State Laws

The humane officer will probably be familiar with the local and state laws on animal cruelty. Weak animal anti-cruelty laws can slow down and hamper an investigation so don't always blame the humane officer for being slow to respond in an abuse situation. Most humane officers don't have any more legal rights than you have—they may be ordered off someone's property and charged with trespassing. Fortunately, society has begun to recognize animal abuse as part of the cycle of abuse in families and is now calling for stronger penalties against all abusers. Many states have even added felony penalties to their anti-cruelty laws.

Help to Prevent Neglect and Abuse

The key to preventing neglect is education. Many owners just aren't aware of how important affection is to a pet or even that a puppy can outgrow his collar. For preventing abuse, we need stronger anti-cruelty laws—laws that empower effective enforcement and include harsh penalties. You can help to prevent neglect and abuse by informing others about what to do if they witness such incidents. You can also educate those you know by helping them to better understand how to train and care for their pets. The following are suggestions for preventive education:

- Schedule a speaker from your local humane agency to talk to members of your club or organization.
- Set up a lecture series at your place of employment concerning animal welfare issues.
- Pick up pet care and behavior pamphlets from your local humane agency to distribute to coworkers or friends with pets.
- Support any initiatives to strengthen your state's anti-cruelty laws.
- Write to your local newspaper and television station whenever animal cruelty stories appear. Tell them you support strong penalties for these abusers.
- Conduct a fundraising event for your local humane agency as a volunteer project. Get all your friends who own pets to become involved.
- Volunteer at your local animal shelter.

Neglect Comes in Many Forms

- Leaving a dog outdoors all the time is cruel and inhumane. The HSUS strongly recommends that all pets be kept indoors with the family. They do not discourage pet owners from letting their dogs spend time outside, as long as their dogs are supervised and under control at all times. Leaving a dog outside, especially chained or otherwise tethered, is extremely detrimental to a dog physically, emotionally, and behaviorally. Dogs need companionship, care, exercise, and attention. Leaving a dog outside for an extended period of time without supervision not only deprives him or her of these things, but can also lead to behavior problems—including aggression. It can also put the dog in serious physical danger. A confined dog is unable to escape the harsh effects of weather, such as heat, cold, storms, etc.
- Not grooming a dog or cat—especially long-haired ones—leads to massive matting which causes terrible misery and sores.
- Not increasing the size of the collar as the dog or cat grows can lead to injury, and ultimately death if not dealt with in time.
- Mange, caused by tiny parasites, forces pets to suffer from horrendous itching, loss of hair, and possibly sores caused by scratching and biting as the pet tries to relieve the incessant irritation.
- Starvation is not just caused by lack of food, but by improper food, untreated disease, and parasites such as worms.
- Leaving a pet in a car on a warm day can be a deadly mistake. The temperature in a car can reach 160 degrees in a matter of minutes—even with partially opened windows. The pet can suffer brain damage or die from heatstroke. Signs of heat stress are heavy panting, glazed eyes, rapid pulse, dizziness, vomiting, and a deep red or purple tongue. You can do the following things to help an animal that has been in a closed up car:
    - Get the animal to shade and apply cool water all over his body.
    - Apply ice packs or cold towels to the head, neck, and chest only.
    - Give the animal small amounts of cool water to drink.
    - Get the animal to a veterinarian right away.

PREVENTIVE MEASURES OF ANIMAL CARE

- Don't let your dog travel unsecured in an open pickup truck bed. Dogs can't hold on the way humans can, and any sudden start, stop, or turn can toss your pet onto the highway.
- Most dogs love the feeling of wind blowing past their ears at 60 mph, but that wind can seriously irritate mucous membranes and blow

pieces of grit into the animal's eye, which could cause permanent damage to the eye. Insects or flying debris can also lodge in the nasal passages or get sucked up into the windpipe.
- Do not leave dogs or cats outdoors when the temperature sharply drops. Short-haired, very young, or old dogs and cats should never be left outdoors. Short-coated dogs may feel more comfortable wearing a sweater during walks.
- Warm engines in parked cars attract cats. To avoid injury or death, bang on car hoods to scare them away before starting engines.
- Salt and chemicals used to melt snow and ice can burn the pads of pets' feet. Wipe them with a damp towel before animals lick them and burn their mouths.
- Antifreeze tastes sweet but is deadly poison to pets and children. Wipe up spills and store all household chemicals out of reach.

Contact your veterinarian or local animal hospital immediately if your pet is injured or ill. It is important to have your veterinarian's phone number easily accessible in case of an emergency.

PREVENTING ANNOYING PET HABITS

While our pet's behavior(s) may be annoying to us, it is perfectly normal for a cat or dog. The following are some simple solutions to problems—the kind of problems that may lead one to abuse their pet without realizing it. Pet owners usually punish their pets for behaving in a way that is natural to the animal. Try these cures! They do work!

When Your Pet Eats Your Plants

Although our pets are basically carnivores, grass and plants are part of the regular diet of free-roaming cats and dogs. To prevent your pet from eating your plants:

- Use black pepper, hot sauce, or other foul-tasting substances sold at your local pet store.
- Keep plants out of their reach.
- Try giving your pet some vegetables in their diet, such as lettuce, green beans, and carrots.
- Cats, in particular, love to eat plants so give your cat his or her own "kitty plant" consisting of grass.

When Your Dog Chases Cars

Chasing cars (or any other moving object) can be very dangerous to all involved. Researchers still have not yet figured out why some dogs do this. The first thing to do when your pet chases an object is to enroll them in an obedience class so that he or she learns to stay put when distractions occur. Take your pet to places where there are cars, bicycles, etc., but keep him or her at a safe distance from them. Make sure you have your dog on a leash at all times and use a lot of praise and food rewards for good behavior.

When Your Dog Continually Barks

Some dogs like to bark at almost anything: the doorbell, the telephone, a person walking by your house, another animal in your yard, or any other sound or movement nearby. Some dogs bark when defending their territories. Some bark to get attention or food from their owners. Others will bark when left alone. If your dog is an annoying barker, first try to figure out why. There may be a physical reason for the disturbing bark. If the barking is due to being left alone, consult your veterinarian so that he or she can set up a behavior modification program to help your dog. This type of program involves a series of short departures to teach your dog not to be anxious when left alone.

When Your Pet Tries to Escape Through an Open Door

For dogs, the solution is a simple one. Before opening the door, always ask your dog to sit or stay. Be sure to praise for good behavior. This is more difficult to solve with a cat. Some pet owners have been successful using a spray bottle filled with water. If your cat tries to dart out the door, give him or her a squirt. After you do this a few times, your cat will learn to stay put.

When Your Dog Nips at Heels

This behavior is more common in dogs bred to herd sheep and cattle, such as sheepdogs and collies. To break this habit, use the same solution used to keep dogs from chasing moving objects. Teach your dog to sit or stay and be sure to praise and reward with dog treats. Have people walk by him or her at a slow pace. Then gradually reduce the distance between the dog and the person and quicken the pace. Praise him for not nipping when the person goes by. If the dog does attempt to nip, jerk quickly on the leash. Refrain from running from your dog since this will only enhance the behavior.

Unfortunately, many pet owners abuse their pets for behaviors such as these when it would only take a little time and some tender loving care to solve the problem. Many pets are taken to animal shelters because the owners cannot or will not take the time to train their pet. Some are just abandoned because the owner gives up. Please take some time to train your pet or consult your veterinarian for advice.

A SERIOUS ISSUE

Unfortunately, animal abuse has not stopped. Offenders are at schools, college campuses, adults, children—all who know better than to abuse innocent animals. It is important that people be aware of such cases so that man is aware of the need for protective action.

- According to the Animal Defense League Fund (ADLF), two college baseball players attending Baylor University in Waco, Texas, allegedly shot, skinned, and beheaded a cat named Queso. Clint Bowers and Derek Brehm were charged in the death of the cat and suspended from Baylor for 15 days.
- In Brea, California, 85 children, ages ranging from kindergarten through 12th grade, witnessed a cow being slaughtered at Carbon Canyon Christian School, according to People for the Ethical Treatment of Animals (PETA) Action Alerts. The rationale for having the students witness this cruel act was so they could see it instead of only experiencing it through the books they had read during the school year.
- A Winston County, Alabama man, William Robinson, in September 2000, allegedly shot his Labrador mix puppy and burned the dog on a burning trash pile, while it was still alive. Neighbors were unable to rescue the screaming wounded puppy, which burned to death. Robinson stated he shot and burned the puppy for getting into the trash.
- Two 13-year-old boys, according to a PETA Actionline Report, sodomized a kitten who followed them with a stick. According to witnesses, the kitten tried to run away but the boys picked her up and threw her to the ground as well as swinging and shaking her violently. While the cat was trying to escape by climbing a tree, the boys followed her and shoved a stick into the kitten. The kitten's anus was ruptured, and she had internal injuries and neurological damage when brought to Pasado's Safe Haven of Shnohomish County, Washington State.

- Hop Bottom, Pennsylvania was the scene of a tame deer, Bam Bam, that was shot and killed. Richard L. Groover, 52, shot and killed Bam Bam, a four-year-old tame male deer confined in a fenced-in area. The deer had been raised by Nancy Pordon since infancy. Instead of being charged with a felony crime, Groover was able to plead guilty to a lesser charge of criminal mischief and firing a firearm within a safety zone.

As disturbing and cruel as these reports are, it is important that humans be aware of the cruelty that fellow humans inflict on innocent animals. These innocent animals will have no protection and justice unless we are aware of the need and act on it.

HUMANE EDUCATION

No single person or group can be blamed for dog and cat overpopulation—overall responsibility is shared by many segments of the public. The source of the problem includes accidental mating, breeding for the purpose of selling the offspring, and personal reasons like, "I want my children to witness the miracle of birth." Pet owners who do not spay or neuter their animals are the greatest single cause of the companion animal tragedy. Many of these owners have no intention of breeding their pets, but it happens. Allowing your pet to have just one litter so your children can experience the miracle of birth can contribute to thousands of unplanned births. This is what can happen: two dogs breed. Six offspring are born. The six offspring reproduce within one year and are responsible for six offspring each. In one year a litter of six can become 36. Unfortunately, it doesn't stop there! (The Fund for Animals, Companion Animal Fact Sheet #1). To solve the problem we must prevent animals from being born unnecessarily. There are three measures society can take to help prevent the overpopulation of animals:

- humane educational programs
- affordable and accessible spay/neuter clinics
- enforcement of laws (i.e., mandatory licensing and leash laws).

Because both approaches must be taken concurrently, it is critical that our efforts to educate the public about the problem increase. Animal shelters are doing the public's difficult work. They care for the animals people discard, and must destroy those for whom no homes can be found. We, the public, must take responsibility for animals ending up in shelters. We can do this in the following ways.

Educational Programs

Programs must be developed for adults, because adults are responsible for dogs and cats. At the same time, we must reach children and young adults. By teaching children how to be caring and responsible animal guardians early, it is hoped they will grow to be more sensitive and responsible adults—adults who create a more compassionate world for all.

Spay/Neuter Clinics

Low cost spay/neuter clinics provide an affordable solution. Spaying is a surgical technique performed on females. It involves removal of both ovaries and the uterus. The operation prevents an animal from having heat periods and eliminates the ability to become pregnant. Neutering is a surgical technique performed on male animals involving removal of the testicles. This prevents production of sperm and eliminates the possibility of the male impregnating the female. Both surgeries are usually performed at six months of age; however, many clinics are now sterilizing animals at an earlier age. If you have specific concerns about spaying/neutering, consult with your veterinarian for advice.

What You Can Do

The Fund for Animals is committed to finding new and innovative ways to solve this crisis. You can help to end overpopulation of animals by:

- Spaying or neutering your dogs and cats and encouraging others to do the same.
- Adopting from your local animal shelter. All shelters are overloaded with adoptable animals who need homes.

Spay Day USA is a national campaign of the Doris Day Animal Foundation. Its purpose is to:

- Raise the public's awareness of the severe companion animal overpopulation problem—particularly of cats and dogs—in the United States.
- Promote spay/neuter surgery as a primary means of addressing companion animal overpopulation.

- Inspire each American to take personal responsibility for preventing the births of unwanted litters by sponsoring the spay or neuter of at least one companion animal or untamed cat.

On Spay Day USA, the last Tuesday of February, veterinary clinics, humane organizations, and concerned citizens all across the country join forces to promote spay/neuter as a responsible, humane method of solving the overpopulation problem. Many local groups celebrate Spay Day USA during the weekend before or after this day, during the entire last week of February, or during the entire month of February and sometimes March. Spay Day USA first took place in 1995 and was sponsored by the Doris Day Animal League. In 1998, Spay Day USA became a program of the League's sister organization, the Doris Day Animal Foundation. Since its beginning, it is estimated that about one half million animals have been altered in conjunction with Spay Day. When you consider that two unaltered cats and all their descendants, if none are ever altered, can number 420,000 in seven years, while two unaltered dogs and their descendants can number 67,000 in just six years, it is clear that Spay Day USA has been successful in preventing millions of unwanted births.

Every day, there are things you can do to be animal's best friends:

- Encourage friends and neighbors to join you in donating food, blankets, towels, and time to your local animal shelter.
- Avoid purchasing products that were tested on animals.
- Share your love for animals and how to properly care for them with children. Our greatest legacy will be a more animal friendly world.

Combine your voice with others and you can make a real difference in the lives of all animals by ensuring that they have the legal protection they need to save them from those who would cause them unspeakable harm.

At Twice the Price

A man was on the side of the road with a large birdcage. A boy noticed the cage was full of birds of many kinds.

"Where did you get those?" he asked.

"Oh, all over the place," the man replied. "I lure them with crumbs, pretend I'm their friend, then when they're close, I net and shove them into my cage."

"And what are you going to do with them now?"

The man grinned, "I'm going to prod them with sticks and get them really mad so they fight and kill each other. Those that survive, I'll kill. None will escape."

The boy looked steadily at the man. What made him do such things? He looked into the cruel, hard eyes. Then he looked at the birds, defenseless, without hope. "Can I buy those birds?" The boy asked.

The man hid a smile, aware that he could be on to a good thing if he played his cards right. "Well," he said hesitantly, "The cage is pretty expensive and I spent a lot of time collecting these birds. I'll tell you what I'll do. I'll let you have the lot, birds, cage, and all for 10 pounds and that jacket you're wearing."

The boy paused—10 pounds was all he had and the jacket was new and very special—in fact, it was his prized possession. Slowly, he took out the 10 pounds and handed it over. Then even more slowly he took off his jacket, gave it one last look and then handed that over, too.

"Thank you very much," the man said. "What are you going to do with all these birds now?" The man stood watching in disbelief, a muffled utterance escaping his lips as the child opened the door to release the birds. Looking up into the eyes of the hardened man, the small child commented in response, "Hate holds on, while Love lets go."

—Author Unknown

Of all the animals, man is the only one that is cruel. He is the only one that inflicts pain for the pleasure of doing it.

—Mark Twain

Until he extends the circle of compassion to all living things, man will not himself find peace.

—Dr. Albert Schweitzer

The Problem of Pain

The problem of animal suffering is appalling; not because the animals are so numerous (for . . . no more pain is felt when a million suffer than when one suffers) but because the Christian explanation of human pain cannot be extended to animal pain. So far we know, beasts are incapable, either of sin or virtue: therefore they can neither deserve pain nor be improved by it. At the same time we must never allow the problem of animal suffering to become the center of the problem of pain; not because it is unimportant— whatever furnishes plausible grounds for questioning the goodness of God is very important indeed—but because it is outside the range of our knowledge. God has given us data which enable us, in some degree, to understand our own suffering: He has given us no such data about beasts. We know neither why they were made nor what they are, and everything we say about them is speculative. From the doctrine that God is good we may confidently declare that the appearance of reckless Divine cruelty in the animal kingdom is an illusion—and the fact that the only suffering we know at first hand (ours) turns out not to be a cruelty will make it easier to believe this. After that, everything is guesswork. . . .

We have reason to believe that not all animals suffer as we think they do: but some, at least, look as if they had selves, and what shall be done for these innocents? And we have seen that it is possible to believe that animal pain is not God's handiwork but begun by Satan's malice and perpetuated by man's desertion of his post: still, if God has not caused it, He has permitted it, and, once again, what shall be done for these innocents?

—*C. S. Lewis,* On Grief, *1979, p. 56*

A Dog's Plea

Treat me kindly, my beloved friend, for no heart in all the world is more grateful for kindness than the loving heart of me.

Do not break my spirit with a stick, for though I should lick your hand between blows, your patience and understanding will more quickly teach me the things you would have me learn.

Speak to me often, for your voice is the world's sweetest music, as you must know by the fierce wagging of my tail when your footstep falls upon my waiting ear.

Please take me inside when it is cold and wet, for I am a domesticated animal, no longer accustomed to bitter elements. I ask no greater glory than the privilege of sitting at your feet beside the hearth.

Keep my pan filled with fresh water, for I cannot tell you when I suffer thirst.

Feed me clean food that I may stay well, to romp and play and do your bidding, to walk by your side, and stand ready, willing and able to protect you with my life, should your life be in danger.

And, my friend, when I am very old and I no longer enjoy good health, hearing, and sight, do not make heroic efforts to keep me going. I am not having any fun. Please see that my trusting life is taken gently. I shall leave this earth knowing with the last breath I draw that my fate was always safest in your hands.

—*Author Unknown*

CHAPTER 15
Healing Activities

> Do not seek death. Death will find you. But seek the road which makes death a fulfillment.
> —*Dag Hammarskjold*

In our society we are expected to "get over" the death of a pet almost immediately, yet often this tragedy is felt as strongly as if a human family member had died. This feeling of loss can be intense enough to cause emotional and physical reactions and disturbances. How we react and what we do in regard to this loss can have long-term effects on our lives. The most important thing to remember is that your pet has been a very important part of your life and now you must readjust your daily routine. This does not happen immediately, so give yourself time to mourn the death of your faithful and devoted friend.

People tend to suppress or hide their feelings of sadness and pain because of embarrassment or fear of rejection by their family, friends, or co-workers. By not accepting and dealing with these feelings, you allow the pain to go unresolved. Your attitude and behavior reflect this hidden pain. Unresolved conflict or grief stays with us and manifests itself often in negative ways. It may cause problems in other relationships you have or may interfere with your job, such as lack of concentration. There may be physical reactions such as numbness, shortness of breath, heavy chest, and tightness in throat. Anger, fear, guilt, panic, depression, and loneliness are some of the emotional reactions to grief. Spend time with family members who are also grieving. Comfort each other. Think of all the memories you have together with your pet. Talk and cry. It's good for the soul!

The bond between pet and human is often a very deep and loving one. When a pet dies or is lost for whatever reason, humans are most often at a loss as to how to deal with the emotions and pain that accompany this sad event. Counseling can help guide you through the grief process and provide information about dealing with the loss and, as the healing continues, help establish new relationships and daily routine in life.

One of the best remedies for healing pain and grief is that of journaling—putting your feelings, thoughts, and experiences down on paper will give you the opportunity to work through the pain and sorrow. Many people don't think they have the capacity to write—that it's something for professionals or those with creative talents. However, writing is one of the most powerful techniques you were given for expressing your feelings and working through your emotions. Open yourself up on paper. Express your pain and grief in words. It's cathartic—cleansing to the body and mind! You will release the negative emotions you are harboring inside—eating at you every moment and consuming your soul. Venting your emotions through writing will help to set you free. Trust me! Start with the writing activity below and then do those that follow as you continue through your grief work.

ACTIVITY #1—JOURNAL WRITING

Begin by writing for five minutes the first day. Put down on paper your thoughts about your pet. After five minutes put the paper aside. On the next day, write for ten minutes doing the same thing you did the day before. On the third day and every day thereafter, write for 15 minutes. Discipline yourself to write even on those days you don't feel like writing. This is part of the grief work. If you need help getting started, begin your writing with, "I remember when," or "I feel." On the first day, you may want to write about the good times and then the bad times, and finally, the death of your pet. Each time you sit down to write, keep the pen or pencil moving at all times. Write without thinking—freeing your emotions and feelings. Write whatever you want. Don't worry about what others will think and be as specific as possible as often as you can. Describe in detail. Don't worry about spelling or grammar—you are not writing for a grade. Don't try to be creative—leave that for the professionals! As the days go on and you wish to write longer than 15 minutes, go for it! Turn your writings into a story. Add pictures if you wish and give it a title. Keep your masterpiece as a memorial to your pet. And, who knows, someday you might want to publish it as a book for children or add it as a "personal story" to someone else's book! Good luck in your journaling experience!

ACTIVITY #2—ANGER LIST

Repressed anger can become a potent force in self-destructiveness. Release it now and let it go. This is a difficult task and requires you to be honest with yourself. This activity will take a few days to complete so get paper and pencil and start to work right away!

Write the word "ANGER" at the top of the page. Under the word "anger" write down the names of all the people with whom you are angry. These are people who you feel have upset you in any way during your bereavement. Leave a few lines under each name so you can add more information.

After you have written down all the names of the people who have angered you, go back and fill in the reasons why they made you angry. Omit your name from this list.

Now, make a second list with the names of agencies, institutions, situations, or anything else you feel is guilty in causing you unnecessary anger and pain during your bereavement.

Put the list away for three days before reading it again. Take this list out again and see how your feelings have changed. Time can give you greater objectivity! Make notes next to each name. Did your anger lessen or worsen? Are you surprised at the way you feel after three days? Examine your list again in another three days and see if you notice any further changes.

ACTIVITY #3—WRITE A EULOGY

Write a eulogy for your beloved pet. Tell about all the good times and happiness you shared. Talk about your pain and loss. Have a memorial service and invite those who cared about and/or loved the animal. Read your eulogy aloud.

ACTIVITY #4— CELEBRATION OF LIFE SCRAPBOOK

Preserve your memories by celebrating your pet's life in a scrapbook. You and your family can express your grief together throughout the pages. Have the children draw pictures of the pet. Write stories and poems. Add photos and special mementos. Start your scrapbook off with a story about your pet. The following list will help to get you started!

- Identify your pet (name, type of animal, breed, sex, and age).
- Describe how you got your pet (gift, found, adopted, or purchased by you).
- What were your thoughts and/or feelings about your pet when you first got it?
- Why did you choose the name you gave your pet?
- Describe three special moments you and your pet experienced together.
- Describe the kind of relationship you had with your pet (friend, soulmate, member of the family).
- Did your pet teach you any lessons in life? If so, what are they?
- If you had your pet euthanized, describe the experience. How did you make the decision? Did you stay with your pet? Did you have any guilt feelings? If so, explain.
- Describe your feelings and/or emotions when your pet died. Did you find yourself in shock and unable to believe that your pet was gone? Did you ever feel like from everyone? Were you angry at yourself or others? If so, how did you express your anger?
- Did you try to bargain with God or others to allow your pet to live longer?
- Was the sadness ever overwhelming or paralyzing?
- Have you accepted the death of your pet?
- Describe the disposition of your pet (buried, cremated, etc.).
- Did you have prayers, rituals, ceremonies, etc.?
- Describe what you did with your pet's personal belongings.
- What have you done with the photographs of your pet?
- If you have other animals around your house, describe how they reacted when your pet died.
- Did they seem to notice that the pet was gone?
- What expressions of grief did they display?
- Describe how you coped with your grief and pain.
- What helped you to work through your bereavement (support group, counseling, friends, yourself)?
- What has helped you overcome the pain?
- What have you learned from the death of your pet?

ACTIVITY #5—CREATE A COLLAGE

Create a collage with pictures of your pet. Cut out words and phrases from magazines and newspapers that describe your pet and add them to the collage.

ACTIVITY #6—PET GENOGRAM

Draw a diagram of your pet family showing all the pets you have ever had (including the one[s] that are still alive). Use circles for females and squares for males. If a pet is deceased, color in the circle or box to show this information. You can set this up in any fashion you wish. A simple diagram would be a line drawn from left to right with your birth year on the left and the present year on the right. In between you add lines for each pet—including their name, the years you had them, how they died, etc. Be as creative as you wish!

ACTIVITY #7— PET JOURNAL FOR CHILDREN

This journal is about you and your special pet. Get a spiral notebook or journal to begin the story about the life of your pet. Give your book a title and set it up in any way you want. You might want to cut out letters from magazines or newspapers that spell out your pet's name and place it on the first page with a picture of your pet. You might see other pictures that remind you of your special little friend that you can add to your book. Below are questions and activities to do in honor of your pet, so have fun and enjoy the memories!

- What is your pet's name?
- What kind of animal was your pet?
- What color was your pet?
- How much did your pet weigh?
- How big was your pet?
- How old was your pet when you got it?
- How old was your pet when it died?
- How did your pet die?
- Were you with your pet when it died?

Write something after each statement below.

- My pet and I used to . . .
- I wish I could . . .
- My favorite activity with my pet was . . .
- I feel . . .
- I wonder . . .
- A special day was when . . .

- I would like to . . .

>Draw a picture of your pet.

>Pets die for many different reasons. List or draw some reasons why pets die.

>Draw a picture about why your special pet died.

>Write a story about the picture you drew.

You probably have a lot of feelings about the death of your pet. And, sometimes you probably think other people just don't understand how you feel. You might even be afraid of death. You may not want to see it or hear about it. And, you may not want to talk about it. You might pretend that death does not matter to you. What is it about death that makes you afraid?

Think about the last time you were afraid. Draw a picture of when you were afraid.

>Give your picture a title.

>Write about how sad you felt when your pet died.

>Did you cry when your pet died?

It is okay to cry. Tears are a good way to let go of some of your feelings. Draw a picture of yourself when you were sad about your pet dying.

>Give your picture a title.

You may think that you caused your special friend to die. But, you need to know that this is not really true. The things we think about cannot make someone die. The things we say cannot make someone die. Remember, death is not your fault! Do you have any questions about why your pet died?

When our pet dies, it means he or she cannot come back to life. This means he or she no longer breathes or eats. All you have left are your memories. They are yours to keep forever and ever. Draw a picture of the best memory about your pet.

>Give your picture a title.

Maybe you did not get a chance to say good-bye to your pet before he or she died. This may hurt you a lot. But now is your chance to write a letter to your special friend, telling him or her what you never had the chance to say before.

Talking about your pet with someone will help to make you feel better. Write the names of three people you can turn to when you want to talk about your pet.

Create your own "Pages of Memories" in your book. You can use crayons or colored pencils to draw pictures. You can make pictures out of construction paper. You can cut out words or pictures from magazines. You might want to put some stickers on it, too. When you are having a special memory about your pet, make something to add to your memory pages. Use tape or glue to attach your items. Add flowers on holidays or special days throughout the year. Be creative. You can add whatever you want to make your memories come alive.

MAGGIE MAE TRENT, 1991-2000

Maggie was almost ten years old when we had to put her to sleep in November of 2000. That was one of the hardest decisions we've ever

Maggie

had to make. But I realize that she is in a much better place and no longer suffering.

Maggie was a very special dog. She was a purebred Cocker Spaniel and we bought her from a couple when she was about a year old. We wanted a dog that was already housebroken so we were looking for something around a year old. Well, she seemed perfect! What we found out afterwards just made me sick. Apparently, the other two big dogs that she used to live with tossed her around like a rag doll, and her owners were not home much of the time so she was fending for herself against the two big dogs. That explained some of the quirks that Maggie had like grabbing a mouth full of food and running away to eat it even though she had no competition in her new, loving home. She was also very skittish and did not like to be touched or petted on the top of her head. Because she had had a very bad first year of life, I overcompensated with gentle love and understanding for her.

We battled for almost a year to keep her alive. She had kidney failure, and an autoimmune problem, which made her allergic to herself. She would break out in sores all over her skin and eventually lose the hair on her back. I used to tease her that she would be the first hairless Cocker Spaniel. She was on various medications and I was taking her to the vet at least twice a month.

During her last few weeks she became very ill and could barely walk. I would carry her outside to do her business. My husband and I had to make a decision. We felt it was unfair to put her through any more unnecessary pain and suffering, so I made the dreaded call to our vet and told him we thought it was time. I asked him when we could do it and he said he would do it anytime we were ready. We decided to do it the same day I called the vet at around 5:00 in the afternoon. I left work early to spend a few hours with my Maggie. I sat on the couch and she sat right beside me on her special blanket the whole time until my husband came home. I think she knew. Even then, she didn't get up because she was so sick. He came in and said it was time and started to take Maggie from me. I told him "no," I would take her to the car. I carried her out to the car and laid her down in the back seat and gave her a kiss goodbye. I could not go to the vet with my husband. I wasn't strong enough. He stayed with her until she was gone. I cried a lot of tears and from time to time; I still do, like I am right now while trying to write this. I know this is the best thing we could have done for our Maggie.

I stayed home from work the next day and cried all the while I was getting rid of her things. I just didn't want any reminders right now. We had already decided we wanted to get another pet after Maggie was gone, and this time we want a puppy. I didn't want to wait, so within a week I had already purchased new dog toys, dishes, and crate for training. I had everything except for our new puppy. A few days later we found our new puppy and she was only 11 weeks old. We brought her to her new home, which was already set up. The people we bought her from had already named her Casey, and since she responded to the name, and we like it, we decided to keep it. Casey is now a little over a year and she is the queen of the house. She has stolen our hearts. I have never forgotten Maggie, because she will always be a very special memory to me. I always said that Casey was not a replacement for Maggie—she was an addition to our family. I often tell Casey when she does something that reminds me of Maggie. This helped us get over our loss of Maggie, but we will never forget her.

—*Cheryl Trent, personal communication*

DON HO'S LITTLE SCOOTER MAN

In the early 1980s, my husband and I had just returned from spending two long, hot years in the Middle East. While we were working there, we had both been deprived of so many things, especially contact with the living, breathing people and pets we loved and missed. He had been separated from his two pre-teen children who lived with his

Scootie

ex-wife, and I had given up a beloved cat into the care of my sister while I was away. So, we both had a lot of emptiness in our hearts that needed filling.

One day while walking through a mall in Columbia, South Carolina, we wandered into a pet shop. I had always had a dog or cat throughout my entire life and simply enjoyed looking at the pets in the window, even though I never had any serious intention of acquiring another. However, he confided to me that he had always wanted a dog while he was growing up, but his mother had never allowed him to have one. For some reason, our attention was drawn to one particular puppy who appeared to be somewhat older than the others. He was a strawberry blonde and white color and had beautiful, long, floppy ears. When the attendant offered to let him out of his cage so we could have a closer look, my knees felt weak, and my heart started to race. I though, "Uh, oh!" My husband said he had always wanted a Cocker Spaniel just like that one, and although I half-heartedly tried to discourage him, because I knew owning a pet was a major commitment, we ended up taking him home with us that very day. On the way home, I held him in my lap, and could feel his little heart racing also. He seemed just as afraid of going with us as we were of taking on the responsibility of raising him.

The next few months proved to be very tumultuous, and it was quite an adjustment for all of us. However, once we made the commitment that Scootie would be sharing our lives for a number of years to come, things began to settle down to a routine. We ended up moving to Charlotte, North Carolina, for three years before relocating to Florida in 1985. Of course, Scootie made all the moves with us, and although I would never had admitted it at the time, to me he became the child I'd never had. Although he was officially my husband's dog, I had no idea I could grow to love a pet so much. After moving to Florida, I came home every day at lunch time to walk him, and when I returned at night, he would always be waiting at the door for me.

As the years passed and Scootie started to age, he developed some physical problems. His eyesight began to fail, his joints became stiff, and his heart began to tire. Oh, what a difficult time this was for me because I knew he wouldn't be around too much longer. As Scootie was aging, our marriage also began to fail and finally ended in divorce. My husband moved out, leaving the dog with me. (His new-found love already had a dog, he said.) I am so very glad that he did leave Scootie with me, because I don't know how I ever would have survived the divorce if he hadn't been there for me. Although it has been almost ten years, I still remember how I held him and cried every night over my lost marriage. I felt as if I had lost everything—especially my security and my lifestyle. Scootie would sit very still while I cried or sometimes he would nuzzle my face—he seemed to understand that I was going through a very difficult time. What a comfort that dog was to me, since I had no family here in Florida, and I didn't seem to have any real friends left after the divorce.

One of the saddest days of my life was about five years ago when I had to make that dreaded decision to put Scootie to rest. He was in so very much pain, and the quality of his life had deteriorated drastically as he was approaching 13 years of age. It was a Saturday I'll never forget when my vet and her husband came to take Scootie away forever. I called my ex-husband hoping he would want to come by the house and say goodbye and also to help me get through the terrible ordeal; however, he refused, saying he had a golf tournament. That's when I simply hung up the phone, and I never spoke to him again. I went to a neighbor's house while the vet put my dear little friend to sleep, and not being able to come back into the house for quite sometime, I went to the beach and walked for what seemed like hours, trying to find some justification for what I had to do. At one point I looked up into the sky, and there, out over the ocean, I saw a cloud that looked like—using a bit of imagination—a little dog.

Although I've never gotten over the loss of my Cocker Spaniel, I've finally accepted the fact that I did the right thing by letting him go when I did. I know now he is no longer suffering with the pains of old age. I love you, Scootie.

—Jackie Holloman, personal communication

CHAPTER 16
Happy Endings

> It is good to die before one has done anything deserving death.
> —*Anaxandrides*

The following are stories with happy endings—a pet that almost died but was saved and a heroic tale about an animal that saved someone else. In addition, there are some jokes and silly sayings to make you laugh!

PETS AND GRIEF

A lot has been written about how people grieve over the loss of a pet. I have a story with a little different twist. My mother was a gentle and remarkable woman. Many animals were attracted to her gentle and kind ways. My brother has a golden Labrador named Bridget. Bridget loved my mother and my mother loved Bridget. When Mom would go to visit my brother's family, Bridget would almost knock herself over wagging her tail. She was so excited to see Mom, but she would never jump on anyone. Bridget is very well trained. She would sit next to Mom. She would warm her feet and legs in the winter. Every Sunday afternoon Bridget would sit by the window and wait for Mom to come.

Last January, my mother died. When the funeral procession drove to the church, they went down my brother's street. I saw people out at the curb and thought it was such a nice gesture for my brother's neighbors to pay their respects. As we got closer I could see one of my brother's friends standing in a snowdrift, wearing his kilt, playing Irish songs on his bagpipes. Bridget was standing on all fours next to Kevin. As the hearse passed the house, Bridget sat down. She sat up on her hind paws and she waved one of her front paws at the procession. Kevin had a mouth full of bagpipes and could not have said anything to her. My brother's car was three cars behind mine so the dog was not able to see him either. How did Bridget know that Mom was in that car? Was Bridget saying goodbye? My sister-in-law said that the night before Mom died, Bridget paced the kitchen. Did she know she was about to lose her buddy? That part she could have sensed from the "vibes" my brother was sending that night. How did she know to wave goodbye?

—Marty Deluga, personal communication

Great Truths About Life That Little Children Have Learned

No matter how hard you try, you can't baptize cats
You can't trust dogs to watch your food.
Never hold a Dust Buster and a cat at the same time.

—Author Unknown

A MIRACLE STORY

This is a miracle story about our cat, Papa. Briefly, Papa is a 13-year-old male, gray-striped tabby that has a unique background. He came from Key West, namely Ernest Hemingway's house (hence, the name Papa) 13 years ago. He was beautiful with big green eyes, leopard spots on his belly, and extra toes that I heard so much about! Getting Papa was quite an ordeal. I read an article in Cat Fancy magazine about how one can get a Hemingway cat. So I quickly responded and I was put on a waiting list along with others. Well, three years went by and I forgot all about it until one day I received a call that I was up for the next kitten from the Hemingway house. I anxiously left work early and drove down to Key West. Upon my arrival, I went straight to the Hemingway house and picked up Papa. They charged me $50.00 per extra toe and I received notarized documentation as to his authenticity. I was thrilled. He had huge feet and a real spunky personality.

Well, that trip to Key West was many years ago and to this day, Papa remains my closest companion. His personality is the same, but age and time has caught up with him over the last few years. He became diabetic and he recently has been fighting a severe bacterial infection. Being the typical concerned parents, my husband Mark and I pamper Papa like a child as we do our other two cats, Marky and Penzoil.

The following story I am about to tell is a true miracle. It all started on a Friday evening when I fed the cats and gave Papa his usual insulin dosage. But, because of the strong antibiotics Papa was taking, he lost

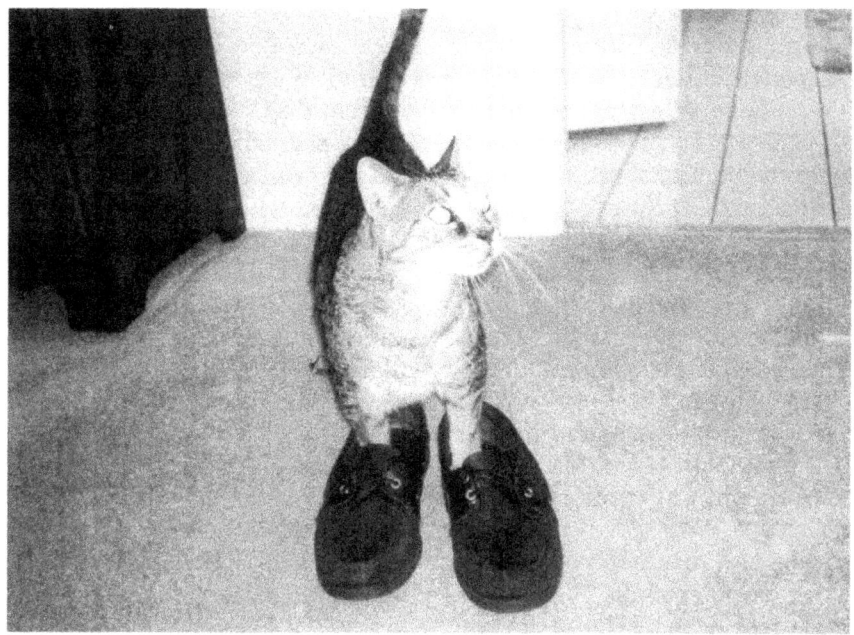

Papa

his appetite and refused to eat. Instead, he ran under our bed to hide. This was not unusual so Mark and I didn't really think much of it because Papa always runs when it's time for his medicine. Apparently, the pill must have had a bitter taste and Papa was not about to take it anymore! Well, we expected Papa to come out eventually to eat. The next morning around 6:00 a.m., my husband awoke from a nightmare so he got up. This is really unusual because Mark seldom dreamed or got up early like that. It must have been fate. Well, he saw Papa's tail sticking out from under the bed and he "flicked" it to play with Papa but Papa did not respond. Mark lifted the covers and yelled aloud to awake me that Papa was dying. I sky-rocketed out of bed and dove to the floor. Papa was catatonic. His cool, lifeless body was becoming stiff and his big green eyes were fixated. Both Mark and I started bawling as I held Papa. But something snapped. My husband said, "No, let's try CPR. We have to do something!?" So, he massaged Papa's chest and, amazingly, Papa's legs kicked! I shrieked and because I was so emotional, kept crying. Mark quickly suggested for me to check the Internet to find out what to do for what appeared to be insulin shock.

I did just that and learned to get anything sweet, such as Karo syrup. The closest thing we had to that was chocolate syrup or orange juice.

Mark proceeded to put some of the chocolate on Papa's gums and I squirted a small amount of juice into his mouth. Papa started responding. We were so excited but we knew that Papa was not out of the woods yet. I rushed to get dressed as Mark phoned the emergency clinic. Driving at fast speed, we flew to the closest animal hospital. As I held Papa close, I kept whispering into his ears and telling him to please hang on! It was obvious that Papa was passing and again, Mark and I were crying aloud. Mark insisted to me that I do mouth to mouth and I told him I never had done that before. He said just do it, so I did . . . and well, unbelievable, Papa's legs started kicking and making a sound! It was a miracle! He came back and was breathing again! Minutes later though, Papa slipped away again. "Oh my God, Papa!" I exclaimed and tried mouth to mouth again. Incredibly, he started kicking again! What an emotional roller coaster! By now, we pulled up to the hospital and ran to their door. They took him in quickly as we waited in the waiting room silently. About a half hour later, the doctor called us in and Papa was stabilized and under Valium to calm his seizures. We were both shocked that he was sill alive! From there, we rushed Papa to our regular vet since the hospital closed early on Saturdays. So, back in the car again, we rushed him there. We dropped him off knowing that still his survival chances were slim. Crying all the way home, my husband and I discussed the possibility of euthanasia. We soon were home and had only a few hours before we had to go back and pick up Papa or hear of his outcome. When we arrived back at the clinic, we were placed in a private room where we expected the bad news. Minutes later, the doctor came in and told us that Papa was doing better! Our mouths dropped! They soon brought him in and he was staggering a little but he was up and walking! We were told, however, that the first 24 hours were crucial and that we should bring him to the animal hospital where be can be observed over night. This way, they can assist Papa with any seizures or whatever may arise. So, again, back in the car we went to another hospital and dropped Papa off.

Mark and I were both ecstatic but our hearts were so wrenched that we were exhausted. We actually felt numb and our bodies ached all over from hysteria. We went home in silence still not knowing if Papa would make it through the night. Sunday morning came and I arose early to call the vet. Great news! Papa can come home!!! Mark and I rushed to pick him up. Papa was up, walking around, and gobbling food like he never has before! We were just beside ourselves and shocked over the whole thing. When we got home, Papa walked into the house and stared doing his usual "inspection" as he ran checking the food bowls, almost as if he was making sure that he was really home and not dreaming. His tail was up high, flickering with happiness. Our other two cats, Marky and

Penzoil, though, backed down and hissed, almost as if they had seen a ghost! They kept their distance and watched Papa closely. It was so bizarre. Perhaps the other cats sensed that Papa had passed on and came back to life. It really appeared that they knew something we didn't. . . .

Well, it has been a few days now and our miracle kitty is alive and happy. The others finally accepted him and things are almost back to normal at home. There are a couple things that Mark and I have noticed since Papa came home. He appears to have had an attitude adjustment. He was always hyper and skittish of loud sounds. Perhaps Papa has seen the "light" because he is so mellow and calm now. He was never that way. He's a new person now. Also, his cry or meow is really low and guttural. He sounds like a lion now! My husband and I truly believe that Papa had the desire to live as we had the love to bring him back. He is living proof that miracles do happen. This experience was the utmost test in our lives. I cannot express enough how much happiness our cats bring to our home and the thought of losing Papa truly was heartbreaking. Papa definitely has nine lives.

—Laura Whyte, personal communication

PUPPY LOVE

A store owner was tacking a sign above his door that read: Puppies for Sale. The signs have a way of attracting children. Soon a little boy appeared at the sign and asked, "How much are you gonna sell those puppies for?"

The store owner replied, "Anywhere from $30.00 to $50.00."

The little boy reached into his pocket and pulled out some change. "I have $2.37. Can I look at them?"

The storeowner smiled and whistled. Out of the kennel came his dog named Lady, running down the aisle of his store followed by five little puppies. One puppy was lagging considerably behind. Immediately the little boy singled out the lagging, limping puppy.

He asked, "What's wrong with that little dog?"

The man explained that when the puppy was born the vet said that this puppy had a bad hip socket and would limp for the rest of his life.

The little boy got really excited and said, "That's the puppy I want to buy!"

The man replied, "No, you don't want to buy that little dog. If you really want him, I'll give him to you."

The little boy got upset. He looked straight into the man's eyes and said "I don't want you to give him to me. He is worth every bit as much as the other dogs and I'll pay the full price. In fact, I will give you $2.37 now and 50 cents every month until I have him paid for."

The man countered. "You really don't want to buy this puppy, son. He is never gonna be able to run, jump, and play like other puppies."

The little boy reached down and rolled up his pant leg to reveal a badly twisted, crippled left leg supported by a big metal brace. He looked up at the man and said, "Well, I don't run so well myself and the little puppy will need someone who understands."

The man was now biting his bottom lip. Tears welled up in his eyes. He smiled and said, "Son, I hope and pray that each and every one of these puppies will have an owner such as you."

Moral of this story: In life, it doesn't matter who you are, but whether someone appreciates you for what you are, accepts you, and loves you unconditionally. A real friend is one who walks in when the rest of the world walks away.

—Author Unknown

Dead Cat Test

A kindergarten pupil told his teacher he'd found a cat. She asked if it was dead or alive.

"Dead," she was informed.

"How do you know?" she asked.

"Because I pissed in his ear and it didn't move." Said the child innocently.

"You did WHAT?!?!" the teacher squealed in surprise.

"You know," explained the boy, "I leaned over and went 'pssst' and he didn't move!"

—Author Unknown

COCO

I had just bought a little Himalayan kitten name Coco and everything seemed to be going fine. He was a sweet little boy who looked like Yoda in Star Wars and had chocolate paws and a smooshed face. I noticed, however, that his stools were loose, and the situation got worse as he got older. Coco had diarrhea twice a day, and the vets were at odds as to what to do. I had to bathe him a lot, and it was very tiring for both of us. One day Coco was bleeding and in absolute pain, and I took him to the vet. The vet and I decided that if he couldn't do anything for Coco, then we would euthanize him as we didn't want him to be in pain anymore. I took pictures of Coco and me together and said my good-byes, as I thought that was the end. Two days later the vet called me and said "Come and take Coco home. He's fine now." I was amazed! It turns out

Coco was allergic to a lot of different foods, and they gave him a type of bacteria (that looked like yogurt) to calm his tummy. After that, they started Coco on special diet, and it's been seven years since! Sure, I regulate what Coco and my other two cats eat, but I don't worry anymore and I treasure every day that I'm with him.

—Elsabe Venter, personal communication

A man brought a very limp dog into the veterinary clinic. As he lay the dog on the table, Doc Burck pulled out his stethoscope, placing the receptor on the dog's chest. After a moment or two, the Doc shook his head sadly and said, "I'm sorry, but your dog has passed away." "What?" screamed the man, "How can you tell? You haven't done any testing on him or anything. I want another opinion!" With that, Doc turned and left the room. In a few moments, he returned with a Labrador Retriever. The Retriever went right to work, sniffing the poor dog on the table and checking him out thoroughly. After a considerable amount of sniffing, the Retriever sadly shook his head and said "Bark." The veterinarian then took the Labrador out and returned in a few moments with a cat, who walked around the poor dog several times and then sadly shook his head and said, "Meow." The cat then jumped off the table and ran out of the room. The veterinarian said, "There's nothing more I can do and handed the man a bill for $600.00 The dog's owner went postal. "$600! Just to tell me my dog is dead? This is outrageous!" Doc shook his head sadly and explained. If you had taken my word for it, it would have been $50.00, but with the Lab work and the cat scan. . . ."

—Author Unknown

BILLY'S MISSION

It was one of the hottest days of the dry season. We had not seen rain in almost a month. The crops were dying. Cows had stopped giving milk. The creeks and streams were long gone back into the earth. It was a dry season that would bankrupt seven farmers before it was through. Every day, my husband and his brothers would go about the arduous process of trying to get water to the farm. Lately, this process had involved taking a truck to the river and filling it up with water. But it was so expensive. Even the river was getting low. If we didn't see some rain soon, we would lose everything. It was on this day that I learned the true lesson of sharing, and witnessed the only miracle I have seen with my own eyes. I was in the kitchen making lunch for my husband and his brothers when I saw my six-year-old son, Billy, walking toward the woods. He wasn't walking with the usual carefree abandon of a youth but with a serious purpose. I could only see his back. He was obviously walking with a great effort, trying to be as still as possible. Minutes after he disappeared into the woods, he came running out again, toward the house. I went back to making sandwiches, thinking that whatever task he had been doing was completed. Moments later, however, he was once again walking in that slow purposeful stride toward the woods. This activity went on for an hour: walk carefully to the woods, run back to the house. Finally, I couldn't take it any longer, and I crept out of the house, and followed him on his journey (being very careful not to be seen, as he was obviously doing important work, and didn't need his Mommy checking up on him). He was cupping both hands in front of him as he walked, being very careful not to spill the water he held in them; maybe two or three tablespoons were held in his tiny hands. I sneaked close as he went into the woods. Branches and thorns slapped his little face but he did not try to avoid them. He had a much higher purpose. As I leaned in to spy on him, I saw the most amazing sight. Several large deer loomed in front of him. Billy walked right up to them. I almost screamed for him to get away. A huge buck with elaborate antlers was dangerously close. But the buck did not threaten him. He didn't even move as Billy knelt down. And I saw a tiny fawn laying on the ground, obviously suffering from dehydration and heat exhaustion, lift its head with great effort to lap up the water cupped in my beautiful boy's hand. When the water was gone, Billy jumped up to run back to the house, and I hid behind a tree. I followed him back to the house, to a spigot connected to an empty tank. Billy opened it all the way up, and a few drops of water began to come out. He knelt there, letting the drip, drip, slowly fill up his makeshift cup, as the sun beat down on his little back. Then it came clear to me: the trouble he had gotten into for playing with the hose the week before, the lecture he had received about the importance of not wasting water, and the reason he didn't ask me to help him. It took a minute for the drops to fill his hands. When he stood up and began the trek back, I was there in front of him. His little eyes just filled with tears. "I'm not wasting," was all he said. As he began his walk, I joined him, with a small pot of water from the kitchen. I let him tend to the fawn. I stayed away. It was his job. I stood on the edge of the woods watching the most beautiful heart I have ever known working so hard to save another life. As the tears that rolled down my face began to hit the ground, they were suddenly joined by other drops—and more drops—and more. I looked up at the sky. It was as if God, himself, was weeping. Some will probably say that this was all just a huge coincidence—that miracles don't really exist—that it was bound to rain sometime. And I can't argue with that. I'm not going to try. All I can say is that the rain that came that day saved our farm, just like the actions of one little boy who saved another.

—Author Unknown

Four men were bragging about how smart their cats are. The first man was an Engineer, the second man was an Accountant, the third man was a Chemist, and the fourth was a Government Worker.

To show off, the Engineer called to his cat, "T-square, do your stuff." T-square pranced over to a desk, took out some paper and a pen and promptly drew a circle, a square, and a triangle. Everyone agreed that was pretty smart.

But the Accountant said his cat could do better. He called his cat and said, "Spreadsheet, do your stuff." Spreadsheet went out into the kitchen and returned with a dozen cookies. He divided them into four equal piles of three cookies each. Everyone agreed that was good.

But the Chemist said his cat could do better. He called his cat and said, "Measure, do your stuff." Measure got up, walked over to the fridge, took out a quart of milk, got a 10-ounce glass from the cupboard and poured exactly eight ounces without spilling a drop. Everyone agreed that was good. The three men turned to the Government Worker and said, "What can your cat do?"

The Government Worker called to his cat and said, "Coffee Break, do your stuff." Coffee Break jumped to his feet, ate the cookies, drank the milk, crapped on the paper, got the other three cats pregnant, claimed he injured his back while doing so, filed a grievance report for unsafe working conditions, put in for Workers Compensation and went home for the rest of the day on sick leave.

—Author Unknown

DOG LETTERS TO GOD

Dear God,

Excuse me, but why are there cars named after the jaguar, the cougar, the mustang, the colt, the stingray, and the rabbit, but not one named for a dog? How often do you see a cougar riding around? We dogs love a nice ride! I know every breed cannot have its own model, but it would be easy to rename the Chrysler Eagle to the Chrysler Beagle!

Dear God,
  We dogs can understand human verbal instructions, hand signals, whistles, horns, clickers, beepers, electromagnetic energy fields, and Frisbee flight paths. What do humans understand?

Dear God,
  Are there dogs on other planets, or are we alone? I have been howling at the moon and stars for a long time, but all I ever hear back is the Beagle across the street.

Dear God,
  How come people love to smell flowers, but seldom, if ever, smell one another? Where are their priorities?

Dear God,
  When we get to Heaven, can we sit on your couch? Or is it the same old story?

Dear God,
  If a dog barks his head off in the forest and no human hears him, is he still a bad dog?

Dear God,
  When my foster mom's friend comes over to our house, he smells like musk! What's he been rolling around in?

Dear God,
  More meatballs, less spaghetti, please.

Dear God,
  Is it true that in Heaven, dining room tables have on-ramps?

Dear God,
  Are there mailmen in Heaven? If there are, will I have to apologize?

Dear God,
  Is it true that dogs are not allowed in restaurants because we can't make up our minds what NOT to order? Or is it the carpets again?

Dear God,
  When my family eats dinner they always bless their food. But they never bless mine. So, I've been wagging my tail extra fast when they fill my bowl. Have you noticed my own blessing?

Dear God,
I've always lived at the shelter and I have everything I need. But many of the cats here have names and I don't. Could you give me a name please? It would be good for my self-esteem.

Dear God,
The new Terrier I live with just peed on the Oriental rug and I have a feeling my family might blame me 'cuz they think I'm jealous of this stupid dog. Since they have no sense of smell, how can I convince them I'm innocent? Does PetsMart sell lie detectors?

—Author Unknown

HOW TO BATHE THE CAT

1. Thoroughly clean toilet.
2. Lift both lids and add shampoo.
3. Find and soothe cat as you carry him to bathroom.
4. In one swift move, place cat in toilet, close both lids and stand on top, so cat cannot escape.
5. The cat will self-agitate and produce ample suds.
   (Ignore ruckus from inside toilet; cat is enjoying this.)
6. Flush toilet three or four times. This provides power rinse, which is quite effective.
7. Have someone open outside door, get on top of the tank and quickly lift both lids.
8. Clean cat will rocket out of the toilet and outdoors, where he will air dry.

Sincerely,
The Dog

—Author Unknown

Glossary

A

Acceptance—the stage in which the bereaved accepts the death of their pet

Afterlife—an existence that follows death

Autopsy—a post-mortem examination of a body to determine the cause of death

B

Bargaining—the stage in which the bereaved psychologically and emotionally accept death, but negotiate with themselves, with others, or with God for more time with their pet

Bereaved—one who suffers the death of a beloved pet

Bereavement counseling—consultation begun after a death to address the physical, emotional, and social impact it has had on survivors

Burial—interment of a dead body

C

Cemetery—a burial ground; graveyard

Columbarium—a structure containing niches for cinerary urns

Complicated mourning—refers to grief reactions or mourning processes that are not only unusual but also abnormal in the sense of being deviant and unhealthy

Cremation—disposal of the dead by incineration

D

Dead—no longer alive; having the physical appearance of death

Death—the state of being dead

Denial—an initial stage of grief in which the pet owner may be unable to believe the death of their pet has occurred

Depression—a stage of grief in which a pet owner remains despondent about the death of a pet

Die—to cease existing

Disenfranchised grief—refers to the grief that persons experience when they incur a loss that is not or cannot be openly acknowledged, publicly mourned, or socially supported

Disposition—the entombment, burial, or cremation of the dead; final placement of human remains

Dying—nearing death

E

Euphemism—words that have the same meaning but express it in ways that seem gentler

Euthanasia—painless inducement of death administered by a veterinarian

Euthanize—to kill an animal for reasons considered to be merciful

F

Funeral—the performance of rites, ceremonies, and customs associated with burial or cremation; an organized, purposeful, time-limited, group centered response to death

G

Grave—an excavation for the burial of a corpse; a burial place

Graveyard—a burial ground; cemetery

Grief—deep mental anguish over the death of a loved one; sorrow

Grief counseling—therapy after a death that addresses its physical, emotional, and social impact on survivors

Grief work—the process of accepting and adjusting to the death of a loved one

Grieve—to mourn

Guilt—a psychological construct based on insecurity or a negative self-evaluation

H

Heaven—the abode of souls granted eternal life

I

IAPC—International Association for Pet Cemeteries

L

Life after death—afterlife; immortality

M

Mausoleum—a large tomb housing above-ground burial of a pet

Memorial—a gravestone; monument erected over the tomb of a saint or martyr

Memorial service—a rite held in place of or in addition to a funeral service, at which the body is not present

Monument—a structure or sculpture erected as a memorial; an inscribed stone or other grave marker

Mortality—the condition of being mortal; subject to death

Mourning—the active process of sharing one's grief with another in adapting to the absence of the loved one and establishing a new identity.

Mummify—to preserve a corpse by embalming or drying

Mummy—a body preserved after death by natural or artificial means

N

Neuter—to remove the testicles of a male animal

P

Posttraumatic Stress Disorder—a mental disorder that may develop in response to psychological or physical trauma

R

Reincarnation—the transmigration of a soul from one body to another at death

S

Sorrow—grief

Soul—the vital and immortal human spirit that separates from the body at death

Spay—to excise the ovaries of a female animal

Spirit—the soul; ghost

Spiritualism—the belief in communication between the living and the dead; communication with the dead

Sympathy—the experience or expression of pity or sorrow for the bereavement of another

T

Taxidermy—a technique for preserving animals and showing them as they looked when alive

Telepathy—communication from one mind to another by extrasensory means

Thanatology—the interdisciplinary study of death-related behavior including actions and emotions concerned with dying, death, and bereavement; the study of the nature and causes of death

Tragedy—a disaster or accident involving loss of life

U

Urn—a container in which the ashes of the dead are stored after cremation

V

Veterinarian—a person trained and authorized to treat animals medically

W

Weep—to mourn or grieve

If Dogs Were Our Teachers

If a dog were your teacher, you would learn stuff like:
When loved ones come home, always run to greet them.
Never pass up the opportunity to go for a joyride.
Allow the experience of fresh air and the wind in your face to be pure
    ecstasy.
When it's in your best interest, practice obedience.
Let others know when they've invaded your territory.

Take naps.
Stretch before rising.
Run, romp, and play daily.
Thrive on attention and let people touch you.
Avoid biting when a simple growl will do.
On warm days, stop to lie on your back on the grass.
On hot days, drink lots of water and lie under a shady tree.
When you're happy, dance around and wag your entire body.
No matter how often you're scolded, don't buy into the guilt thing and pout . . . Run right back and make friends.
Delight in the simple joy of a long walk.
Eat with gusto and enthusiasm.
Stop when you have had enough.
Be loyal.
Never pretend to be something you're not.
When someone is having a bad day, be silent, sit close by, and nuzzle them gently.

—Author Unknown

Sources of Support

The following resources are available to help answer any questions and/or concerns you might have. Please remember that Web sites often change addresses or rapidly become obsolete.

Academy for Veterinary Homeopathy
1283 Lincoln Street
Eugene, Oregon 97401
(503) 342-7665

Accredited Pet Cemeteries Society
139 West Rush Road
West Rush, New York 14543
(716) 533-1685

www.amby.com/kimeldorf/bestfriends.html — *Some of My Best Friends* by Martin Kimeldorf is a heart-warming story of Mickey, Mitzi, and Jack and their impact on the author.

American Animal Hospital Association
Membership Service Center
(800) 883-6301

American Holistic Veterinary Medical Association
2214 Old Emmorton Road
Bel Air, Maryland 21015
(410) 569-0795 or (410) 515-7774 (Fax)

American Society for the Prevention of Cruelty to Animals (ASPCA)
New York City, New York
(212) 876-7700 or (800) 946-4646—put in pin #140-7211 and then own telephone number—calls are returned immediately 24 hours a day

American Society for the Prevention of Cruelty to Animals (SPCA)
New York City, New York
(212) 876-7700

American Veterinary Chiropractic Association
P.O. Box 249
Port Bryon, Illinois 61275
(309) 523-3995

American Veterinary Medical Association
www.avrma.org/care4pets/lossandi.htm

www.anaflora.com/contact-order/prayers.html—animal prayer requests

www.angelbluemist.com—*Portrait of an Angel*

Animal Communication
(413) 774-9977

Animal League Defense Fund (Anti-Cruelty Division)
(503) 231-1602

www.action@aldf.org

www.animaljustice.org—This is a new tool to make our voices heard in the fight for animal justice. The Animal Legal Defense Fund's secure Web site uses the power and immediacy of the Internet to educate and mobilize people who care about animals and want to end cruelty to animals in our communities, unnecessary and painful testing and experimentation, and inhumane living conditions on farms.

Animal Medical Center
510 East 62nd Street
New York City, New York
(212) 838-8100

www.animaltalk.net—animal communicators

www.aplb.org—National clearing house for information on pet bereavement

www.aplb.org/rainbow.htm—*All Pets Go to Heaven* by Wallace Sife, Ph.D. Can you imagine a heaven without pets? Neither can this author!

Argus Institute for Families and Veterinary Medicine
Colorado State University
Fort Collins, Colorado
(970) 491-1242
Argos@colostate.com

Association for Pet Loss and Bereavement (APLB)
P.O. Box 106
Brooklyn, New York 11230
(718) 382-0690

Bide-A-Wee Foundation
New York, New York
(212) 532-6395
Wantagh, New York
(516) 785-4199

Chicago Veterinary Medical Association Hotline
(708) 603-3994
24 hour voice-mail; calls will be returned between 7:00 a.m.–9:00 p.m.

Cloud-Nine Coastal Flights
(831) 386-6268 or (831) 385-4362
cloud9flights@juno.com

College of Cornell University Hotline
Ithaca, New York
(607) 253-3932

Companion Animal Association of Arizona
(602) 995-5885
www.caaainc.org
Support group meetings, information, literature, reading lists, and referral service

Companion Animal Related Emotions (CARE)
University of Illinois
Urbana/Champaign
(877) 394-2273
Tuesday, Thursday, and Sunday—7 p.m.–9 p.m.

Cornell University College of Veterinary Medicine Hotline
(607) 253-3932
www.vet.cornell.edu/public/petloss/
Tuesday-Thursday—6 p.m.–9 p.m.

Delta Society
289 Perimeter Road East
P.O. Box 1080
Renton, Washington 99057-9906
(202) 226-7357 or (800) 869-6898
Offers the following resources at minimal charge: pet loss and bereavement packet, directory of pet loss resources, pet loss packet supplement–mental health professionals, pet loss packet supplement–veterinary professionals, and videotapes on pet loss

www.dogheaven.com—*Dog Heaven*

www.dogshavesouls.com/about.html—*Dogs Have Souls Too* by George and Emily Watson—If you have ever agonized over the decision to euthanize a friend, wondered whether animals have souls, or worried that there might not be an afterlife for them, the uplifting story of this remarkable dog will ease your mind. By sharing their experiences, the authors provide comfort and reassurance to readers: The spirit of Miss Sarah most assuredly does live on.

Doris Day Animal Foundation
227 Massachusetts Avenue, NE, Suite 100
Washington, DC 20002
(202) 546-1761 or (202) 546-2193
www.info@ddaf.org

www.educarepress.com/HBPressRel.htm—*Honey-Bun* by Ivy Waters is a beautiful gift-book about pet loss, and the personal journey through grief was written by Anne Stockton, an 88-year-old painter and scholar living in England.

www.emofree.com—emotional freedom techniques

www.familyvet.com/sleep.htm—*Euthanasia: The Family Veterinarian* helps to answer the dreaded question: When should I put an ill pet "to sleep"?

www.find-it.hypermart.net/reiki.htm—International Reiki Practitioners/ Therapists

Fund for Animals, The
8121 Georgia Avenue, Suite 301
Silver Spring, Maryland 20910
(301) 585-2591
www.fundinfo@fund.org

www.gonetodogstar.com—*Gone to Dog Star*

Humane Society of the United States
2100 L Street, NW
Washington, DC 20037-1598
(202) 452-1100

Iams Pet Loss Support Center
(888) 332-7738
Monday-Saturday—8 a.m.–8 p.m.

International Association of Pet Cemeteries
2845 Oakcrest Place
Land O' Lakes, Florida 34639
(800) 952-5541

International Association for Veterinary Homeopathy
334 Knollwood Lane
Woodstock, Georgia 30188
(770) 516-5954

International Veterinary Acupuncture Society
268 West Third Street, Suite 4
P.O. Box 2074
Nederland, Colorado 80466-2074
(303) 258-3767

Iowa State University
College of Veterinary Medicine
Grief Recovery Hotline
(800) 445-4808
Monday-Friday—9 a.m.–5 p.m.

www.lightning-strike.com/—Lightning Strike Pet-Loss Support Page offers a "cybershoulder" for grieving pet owners.

Marty Tousley
www.griefhealing.com

www.members.aol.com/gkurz007—*Cold Noses at the Pearly Gates* by Gary Kurz— Following the devastating death of a family pet, the author searched for answers to the questions that have perplexed pet owners throughout the ages: Is there an animal afterlife? And will I see my pet again? Through a careful analysis of relevant passages from the Bible, the author supplies answers to these questions and shares thoughts on related topics, such as animal communication.

www.members.aol.com/jsharwell/EUTH.htm—*Time To Let Go* is a guide to euthanasia.

www.members.aol.com/moggycat/rainbow.txt—*Rainbow Bridge, The Animals' Eden and Bright New Star*—Inspirational and reassuring stories and poems to help ease the pain of pet loss for those left behind.

www.members.tripod.com/-Sandtracker/cat-tracks.html—*Pet Loss—Tracks in the Sand* by Liz Brophy provides suggestions for dealing with grief, numerous links to other resources, as well as the opportunity to send (or retrieve) Pet Loss Sympathy Cards.

www.methuen-mspca.org/petcare/html/petloss.htm—*When a Pet Dies: Coping with Loss* is an article from the MSPCA which addresses the concerns and feelings you may experience upon the loss of your pet.

www.microserve.net/~dave/bereave.html—*Bereavement* by Dave and Bonnie Ratcliffe is a collection of comforting works by various poets and authors.

www.netcomuk.co.uk/~asclepus/reikidir.html—*The Reiki Practitioners Directory*

www.newrainbowbridge.com/rbpoem.htm—*The Rainbow Bridge Poem* by Steve Bodofsky was inspired by the Rainbow Bridge story and wrote this beautiful poem.

www.news.ksu.edu/WEB/News/NewsReleases/listpetgrief.html — "Pets can Grieve Over a Loss, Too"—According to KSU veterinarian, Kathy

Graughn, "Losing a loved one can be a difficult and painful experience. It can be just as hard on a pet who has lost an owner or another pet within the home."

Nikki Hospice Foundation for Pets
www.csum.edu/pethospice

Ohio State University Hotline
(614) 292-1823
Monday, Wednesday, Friday—6:30 a.m.–9:30 p.m.

OurPALS
www.216.149.169.246

Pet Heaven, Incorporated (animal memorials)
P.O. Box 1158
Ronkonkoma, New York 11779
(631) 471-7038

Pet Line (800) 564-5704

Pet Loss and Grief Support
www.bestfriends.com
www.creatures.com/
www.petloss.com
www.darkpath.net/seminars
www.dogshavesouls.com
www.egroups.com/subscribe/PetTheftSupport
www.gardensofmemory.com
www.mhsource.com/hy/links.html#Grief
www.nepanetwork.com/keepsakes
www.petloss.com/
www.pet-loss.net
www.superdog.com/petloss.htm

Pet Loss Memorials and Tributes
www.cloud9flights.com (aerial dispersion of remains)
www.everlastingstone.com
www.in-memory-of-pets.com/
www.foreverpets.com
www.petgarden.com
www.petsone.com
www.theurnist.com

Pet Loss Resources
www.griefhealing.com/columnsbooks.htm
www.superdog.com/petloss.htm
www.thunder.prohosting.com/~easyshop

Pet Memorials
www.animalnews.com/memorial/
www.golden-rescue.org
www.petreflections.net

www.postgazette.com/magazine/19980304bleo2.asp - *Sometimes, Grief comes Unexpectedly* by Peter Leo—If you've ever lost a friend, you'll understand the depth of feeling so eloquently expressed in this poignant article.

Rainbow Bridge
www.rainbowbridge.com

www.rdpublishers.com/books/rememberingpets.html—*Remembering Pets* by Gina Dalpra-Berman (author) and Barbara Hoss-Schneider (illustrator) who have created this lovely picture book intended to help young children who have lost a special friend.

www.remembrancecross.com—Remembrance Cross (table top memorial)

Spay Day USA
(888) PET-5911 (738-7911)
www.1888pets911.org

www.storyhouse.org/pat.html—*Smoke* by Pat Mountin is a short story about Smoke, the feline companion with whom she spent 20 years.

Summum Mummification
707 Genesee Avenue
Salt Lake City, Utah 84104
(801) 355-0137
www.webhotep.com

Therapeutic Touch
www.therapeutic-touch.org
www.therapeutictouchnetwk.com
www.therapeutictouch.com

www.trfn.clpgh.org/orgs/animalfriends/nancy.html—*They're Only Ours for a Little While* by Nancy Hanson is a poem dedicated to the memory of Duke and Sam.

Tufts University School of Veterinary Medicine Hotline
(508) 839-7966
Monday–Friday, 6 p.m.–9 p.m.; 24-hour voice-mail—long-distance calls are returned collect
www.tufts.edu/vet/petinfo/petloss.html

University of California
School of Veterinary Medicine
Davis, California
(530) 752-4200 or (800) 565-1526
Weekdays—6:30 a.m.–9:30 p.m., Summer hours: Tuesday–Thursday, same hours

University of Florida
College of Veterinary Medicine
Gainesville, Florida
Pet Loss Support Hotline
(352) 392-4700, ext. 4080
24 hour voice-mail; calls will be returned weekdays 7:00 a.m. –9:00 p.m.
www.neuro.vetmed.ufl.edu/alt_med/petgrief/petloss.htm

University of Minnesota
College of Veterinary Medicine
St. Paul, Minnesota
(612) 624-4747

University of Pennsylvania
School of Veterinary Medicine
Philadelphia, Pennsylvania
(215) 898-4529

Veterinary Institute for Therapeutic Alternatives
15 Sunset Terrace
Sherman, Connecticut 06784
(860) 354-2287

Virginia-Maryland Regional College of Veterinary Medicine
(540) 231-8038
Tuesday and Thursday, 6 p.m.–9 p.m.
24 hour voice-mail; calls are returned at no charge

Washington State University
(509) 335-5704
Monday, Tuesday, and Thursday, 7 p.m.–9 p.m. and Saturday, 1:30 p.m.–3 p.m.
24 hour voice-mail; long-distance calls are returned collect
www.vetmed.wsu.edu/PLHL/index.htm

PHANTOM

After experiencing the recent loss of another nephew, and the sudden illness and death of my beloved pet of eleven years, I was grateful to have a few hours after our class Saturday to reflect on these unfortunate events and grieve privately before driving home.

I returned to the emergency animal hospital in downtown Melbourne where the remains of my cat, Phantom, was after suffering a sudden, fatal illness late Thursday night. I had opted for cremation in the event I had to move again. I couldn't bear to leave him behind. He had been with me for so long and loved me unconditionally. Even when I lived alone I never felt lonely due to the constant companionship of my two cats, Phantom and Hershey.

I was relieved to learn Phantom's ashes would be returned to me in a small, ceramic urn designed for the ashes of cats. I had feared I would get them back in some plastic container and have to transfer the remains into a more appropriate urn. I felt the unnecessary handling of his remains would create more grief and lacked the respect I felt he so deserved.

After leaving the hospital, I decided to take a drive to Rockledge Gardens and buy a plant I could tend and nurture in his memory. There I saw beautiful bromeliad "gardens" displayed in hanging baskets and decided that's what I wanted. I left with three small plants and all the things needed to make my own. On the way home I thought: However sad and unfair it can be sometimes, *life is priceless*. It's to be loved, enjoyed, and celebrated. And that's what I intend to do.

—*Margie A. Hughes, 5/5/03*

Magazines, Journals, and Newsletters

Bereavement Magazine
5125 North Union Boulevard, Suite 4
Colorado Springs, Colorado 80918-2056
(719) 266-0006

Cat Fancy and Dog Fancy
P. O. Box 52864
Boulder, Colorado 80322-2864
(303) 666-8504 or (303) 604-7455 (Fax)

Cats
P. O. Box 56886
Boulder, Colorado 80322-6886
(800) 829-9125 or (303) 604-7644 (Fax)

Death Studies
Taylor & Francis
325 Chestnut Street, Suite 800
Philadelphia, Pennsylvania 19106
(800) 354-1420, ext. 216 or (215) 625-2940 (Fax)

Omega, Journal of Death and Dying
Baywood Publishing, Incorporated
26 Austin Avenue, P.O. Box 337
Amityville, New York 11701
(800) 638-7819 or (631) 691-1270 or (631) 691-1770 (Fax)
E-mail: Baywood@Baywood.com

PetLife   Your Companion Animal Magazine
1227 West Magnolia Avenue
Fort Worth, Texas   76104
(817) 921-9300 or (817) 921-9313 (Fax)

PetLife—Your Companion Animal Magazine
400 South Beverly Drive, Suite 214
Beverly Hills, California   90212
(310) 556-5702

Thanatology Newsletter
Brooklyn College
Brooklyn, New York   11210-2889
(718) 951-5553
thanatdc@aol.com

Wagging Tales—Newsletter of The Humane Society of the Treasure Coast, Inc.
4100 SW Leighton Farm Avenue
Palm City, Florida   34990
(561) 223-8822 or (561) 220-3610 (Fax)
tcpets@aol.com

Pet Memorabilia

Gardens of Memory for Pets—a lovely site with beautiful ideas on planting gardens in memory of your pet
www.gardensofmemory.com

Memory Lane Productions—makers of memorial tribute videos of your pet using your collection of photos, home movie films, video clips, slides, scrapbook items, etc.
www.mlvp.com
(888) 831-0389

Pets in Pastel—original commissioned lifelike oil pastel portraits of your pet
www.petsinpastel.com

Pet Memorial Tree Planting—have a young tree planted in the state of your choice in honor of your pet and receive an official certificate of planting and sympathy letter and card
www.treegivers.com

Picture Yourself!—unique cards and shirts with your pet's photo
www.members.tripod.com/~PictureYourself/index.html

Tlyon Graphics—line art, color pencil, and pen portraiture of your pet
www.geocities.com/Nashville/6450/TLGWEB.html

Whispers in the Heart—makers of beautiful pendants to hold photos of beloved pets
www.whisperintheheart.com/with/

www.WorldbytheTail—offers "clay paws": can make a clay impression of the dead pets paw and then bake and decorate

Christmas at Rainbow Bridge

As the midnight hour approaches on Christmas Eve, a tremendous celebration begins. If you listen closely, you will hear the exuberant sound of Bridgekids preparing for the remarkable moment that comes but once a year. Puppies romp through the tall green grass, chasing butterflies and rolling over and over until fits of giggles bring them to a tumbling stop. The volume increases as kittens, cats, tigers, and lions purr in pure delight while the wings of snow white doves gently caress the air. The babbling brook that runs beneath Rainbow Bridge overflows onto the edge of mossy banks and fins of treasured aquatic life quiver in anticipation of the most joyous event. Nestled in the midst of this happy choir of Bridgekids are the littlest angel tots staring in awe at the majestic Christmas tree adorned with flowing strands of angel hair. Effervescent, twinkling stars seesaw elegantly from the sky and land in glorious harmony upon the stoic limbs of Heaven's most perfect Christmas tree. Swaying to and fro in nearby rocking chairs are grandmothers, grandfathers, parents, aunts, uncles, and loved ones. The sound of their whispered lullabies permeate the air as they sing to tiny angel babies resting quietly in their arms.

Like magic the clock approaches midnight and a great stirring is heard in the distance. Each Bridgekid stops and listens, knowing the time is near, and they choose a fleecy cloud on which to snuggle. The roar of purrs drops to barely an audible hum, the babbling brook ripples hypnotically, and the flutter of downy feathered wings fall silent. Heaven's spirited toddlers climb expectantly upon the laps of angels while babies coo in tranquil unison.

Amidst the warm glow of candlelight that rises from the earth below, the arms of the Bridge Keeper envelop the heavens and into the precious hands of each child and in front of each animal a holy gift is placed. With grand exuberance the ribbons are removed and left to fly on a tender breeze where they dissolve into showers of angel dust. As the golden lids of these heavenly gifts are raised, an amazing aura fills the sky, reaching down to the very core of the earth. Ascending from each and every box is the greatest gift of all . . . unending, unconditional, all-encompassing love. This blessed love gently wraps itself around the cherished souls of heaven, warming their hearts with beacons of radiant light and bringing forth from angels an exquisite chorus. As the clock strikes midnight the distance between heaven and earth is vanished. It is at this very moment on Christmas Eve that the Bridge Keeper, His children, angels, and Bridgekids send a message to their earthly loved ones on the wings of this unbridled love.

Listening carefully with an open heart we will hear the familiar voice of our own angel whisper softly into our ear their Christmas message . . ."Let me share with you this love of mine, always and forever. When you need me know that I am here. I have not left you for I am in your heart where I· belong. Our love is eternal as is the brilliant glow of candlelight that illuminates the path to the heavens and Rainbow Bridge. I wait patiently as do you for our inevitable and glorious reunion. I love you, I love you, I love you."

—Author Unknown

Bibliography

Adamec, C. (1996). *When your pet dies: Dealing with your grief and helping your children cope.* New York: The Berkley Publishing Group.

Akiyama, H., Holtzman, J. M., & Britz, W. E. (1986-1987). Pet ownership and health status during bereavement. *Omega, 17*:2, 187-193.

Alexandrovich, N. P. (1992). As totems at an ancient Buelorussian population, *Abstracts and proceedings, The 6th International Conference on Human-Animal Interactions, Animals and Us,* Montreal, Quebec, July 21-25.

Anderson, M. (1996). *Coping with sorrow on the loss of your pet* (2nd Ed.). Kinston, WA: Peregrine Press.

Antinori, D. (1998). *Journey through pet loss* (audiotape). Basking Ridge, NJ: Yoko Spirit Publications.

Armstrong, R. (1994, March 28). The world is going to the dogs. *Newsweek,* 8.

Attig, T. (1996). *How we grieve: Relearning the world.* New York: Oxford University Press.

Barker, S. B. (1993, Fall). Pet owners no longer grieve alone. *American Counselor, 2*:4.

Barker, S. B., & Barker, R. T. (1988). The human-canine bond: Closer than family ties. *Journal of Mental Health Counseling, 10*:1, 46-56.

Barton-Ross, C., & Baron-Sorensen, J. (1998). *Pet loss and human emotion.* Bristol, PA: Taylor & Francis.

Beck, A. M, Katcher, A. H., & Thomas, E. M. (1996). *Between pets and people: The importance of animal companionship.* West Lafayette, IN: Purdue University Press.

Bowlby, J. (1961). Separation anxiety: A critical review of the literature. *Journal of Child Psychiatry, 1,* 251-269.

Bowlby, J. (1969). *Attachment and loss* (Volume 1) *Attachment.* London: Hogarth.

Bowlby, J. (1973). *Attachment and loss* (Volume 2) *Separation.* London: Hogarth.

Bowlby, J. (1980). *Attachment and loss* (Volume 3) *Loss.* London: Hogarth.

Brown, M. W. (1938). *The dead bird*. New York: HarperCollins Publishers.

Bryant, C. D., & Snizek, W. E. (1993). On the trail of the centaur. *Society, 30*:3, 22-35.

Buscaglia, L. (1982). *The fall of Freddie the Leaf*. Thorofare, NJ: Slack Incorporated.

Butler, C. L., & Lagoni, L. S. (1996). Children and pet loss. In C. A. Corr & D. M. Corr (Eds.), *Handbook of childhood death and bereavement* (pp. 179-200). New York: Springer.

Carrick, C. (1976). *The accident*. Clarion, NY: Seabury.

Carson, U. (1989). Do animals grieve? *Death Studies, 13*, 49-62.

Church, J. A. (1987). *Joy in a wooly coat: Living with, loving & letting go of treasured animal friends*. Tiburon, CA: H. J. Kramer, Inc.

Corr, C. A., Nabe, C. M., & Corr, D. M. (1997). *Death and dying, life & living*. New York: Brooks/Cole.

Cowles, K. V. (1985). The death of a pet: Human responses to the breaking of the bond. In M. B. Sussman (Ed.), *Pets and the family* (pp. 135-148). New York: The Haworth Press.

Cummings, C. (1995). *Cracker still lives here: A story of living, loving, and healing*. Fort Myers, FL: River's Edge Publishing.

Cusack, O. (1988). *Pets and mental health*. New York: The Haworth Press.

DeSpelder, L. A. (1996). *The last dance: Encountering death and dying* (4th Ed.). California: Mayfield Publishing Company.

Dickinson, G. E. (1992). First childhood death experiences. *Omega, 25*:3, 169-182.

Doka, E. (1989). *Disenfranchised grief: Recognizing hidden sorrow*. Lexington, MA: D. C. Heath & Company.

Doka, E. (1995). *Children mourning, mourning children*. Washington, DC: Hospice Foundation of America.

Feinman, J. (1996). *Grief and the young child*. Medford, OR: WinterSpring, Inc.

Feinstein, D., & Mayo, P. *Rituals for living and dying: How we can turn loss and the fear of death into an affirmation of life*. San Francisco, CA: Harper.

Foster-Morgan, K. (1995). *Sunflower mountain*. Toronto, Ontario: Sunflower Publications.

Freud, S. (1957). *The standard edition of the complete psychological works of Sigmund Freud* (Vols. XI and XIV). London: Hogarth.

Friedmann, E., Katcher, A. H., Lynch, J. J., & Thomas, S. A. (1980). Animal companions and one-year survival of patients after discharge from a coronary care unit. *Public Health Reports, 95*, 307-312.

Friedmann, E., Katcher, A. H., Meislich, D., & Goodman, M. (1979). Physiological response of people to petting their pets. *American Zoologist, 19*, 327.

Grollman, E. A. (1967). *Explaining death to children*. Boston: Beacon Press.

Grollman, E. A. (1990). *Talking about death: A dialogue between parent and child* (3rd Ed.). Boston, MA: Beacon Press.

Guntzelman, J., & Riegger, M. (1993, January). Supporting clients who are grieving the death of a pet. *Veterinary Medicine*.

Harris, E. L. (1997). *Pet loss: A spiritual guide*. St. Paul, MN: Llewellyn Publications.

Herman, M. (1956). The relationship between man and dog. *Psychoanalysis Quarterly, 25,* 568-585.

Herriot, J. (1977). *All things wise and wonderful*. New York: St. Martin's Press.

Humane Society of the United States, The (1994). *Pet Overpopulation Facts*.

Hunt, L. E . (1998). *Angel pawprints: Reflections on loving and losing a canine companion*. Pasadena, CA: Darrowby Press.

Johnson, J. (1998). *Remember Rafferty*. Omaha, NE: Centering Corporation.

Karmic, B. J. (1985). The effects on family members and functioning after the death of a pet. In M. B. Sussman (Ed.), *Pets and the family* (pp. 149-162). New York: The Haworth Press.

Kastenbaum, R. J. (1986). *Death, society, and human experience* (3rd Ed.). Ohio: Charles E. Merrill Publishing Company.

Katcher, A. H. (1983). Health and the living environment. In A. H. Katcher & A. M. Beck (Ed.), *New perspectives on our lives with companion animals*. Philadelphia, PA: University of Pennsylvania Press.

Kay, W. J. (Ed.) (1984). *Pet loss and human bereavement*. Ames, IA: Iowa State University Press.

Kay, W. J. (Ed.) (1988). Euthanasia of the companion animal: The impact on pet owners. In *Veterinarians & Society*. Philadelphia, PA: Charles Press.

Kearl, M. C. (1989). *Endings: A sociology of death and dying*. New York: Oxford University Press.

Kiddie, K. M. G. (1977). Pathological mourning after the death of a domestic pet. *British Journal of Psychiatry, 131,* 21-25.

King, M., Quintana, M., Veleba, S., & King, H. (1998). *It's okay to cry*. K & K Communications.

Kipling, R. (1972). *The complete verse*. New York: Doubleday & Company, Inc.

Klass, D., Silverman, P., & Nickman, S. (Eds.) (1996). *Continuing bonds: New understandings of grief*. Washington, DC: Taylor & Francis.

Koplewicz, H. S. (1997). *More than moody: Recognizing and treating adolescent depression*. New York: Putnam Publishing Group.

Kosins, M. C. (1992). *Maya's first rose: Diary of a very special love*. Royal Oak, MN: Open Sky Books.

Kowalski, G. (1997). *Goodbye friend: Healing wisdom for anyone who has ever lost a pet*. Walpole, NH: Stillpoint Publishing.

Kowalski, G., Regan, T., & Wolfe, A. (photographer) (1999). *The souls of animals* (2nd Rev. Ed.). Walpole, NH: Stillpoint Publishing.

Kübler-Ross, E. (1969). *On death and dying*. New York: Collier Books/ Macmillan Publishing Company.

Kübler-Ross, E. (1975). *Death: The final stage of growth*. New York: Prentice-Hall.

Kübler-Ross, E. (1983). *On children and death*. New York: Macmillan.

Kurz, G. (1997). *Cold noses at the pearly gates.* Gary Kurz.

Lagoni, L., & Durrance, D. (1998). *Connecting with clients.* Denver, CO: AAHA Press.

Lagoni, L., Butler, C., & Hetts, S. (1994). *The human-animal bond and grief.* Philadelphia: W.B. Saunders.

Lagoni, L. (1997). *The practical guide to client grief.* Denver, CO: AAHA Press.

Lagoni, L., Butler, C., & Hetts, S. (1996). *Friends for life: Loving and losing your animal companion* (audiotape). Louisville, CO: Sounds True Audio.

Lee, L., & Lee, M. (1992). *Absent friend.* Bucks, England: Henston Ltd.

Lemieux, C. M. (1988). *Coping with the loss of a pet.* Reading, PA: Wallace R. Clark.

Leming, M. R., & Dickinson, G. E. (1990). *Understanding dying, death, & bereavement* (2nd ed.). Orlando, FL: Holt, Rinehart, & Winston, Inc.

Levinson, B. M. (1962). The dog as a "co-therapist." *Mental Hygiene, 46,* 59-65.

Levinson, B. M. (1972). *Pets and human development.* Springfield, IL: Charles C. Thomas.

Lewis, C. S. (1979). *A grief observed.* New York: Bantam Books.

Lewis, C. S. (1998). *Lewis on grief.* Nashville, TN: Thomas Nelson, Inc.

Lindemann, E. (1944). The symptomatology and management of acute grief. *American Journal of Psychiatry, 101,*141-148.

Linn, E. (1986). *I know just how you feel . . . avoiding the clichés of grief.* Cary, IL: Publishers Mark.

Lowe, S. (1993, January). A special bond. *Equus, 183,* 24-28, 30.

Mead, M. (1964). Cultural factors in the cause and prevention of pathological homicide. *Bulletin in the Menninger Clinic, 28,* 11-22.

Meer, J. (1984). Pet theories. *Psychology Today, 18*:8, 60-77.

Montgomery, M., & Montgomery, H. (1991). *Goodbye my friend.* Minneapolis, MN: Montgomery Press.

Montgomery, M., & Montgomery, H. (1991). *A final act of caring: Ending the life of an animal friend.* Minneapolis, MN: Montgomery Press.

Mooney, S. (1983). *A snowflake in my hand.* New York: Delta/Eleanor Friede.

Morehead, D. (1996). *A special place for Charlee: A child's companion through pet loss.* Broomfield, CO: Partners in Publishing.

Nicholson, C. (2000). *Crossing the rainbow bridge.* Liverpool, NY: Carp Cove Press.

Nieburg, H. A., & Fischer, A. (1988). *Pet loss and human bereavement.* Ames, IO: Iowa State Press.

Nieburg, H. A., & Fischer, A. (1996). *Pet loss: A thoughtful guide for adults and children.* New York: Harper Trade.

Oblas-Walshaw, S. (1983). *Consoling bereaved clients.* Proceedings, 12th Annual Seminar for Veterinary Technicians, Western States Veterinary Conference.

Osterweis, M. (Ed.) (1984). *Bereavement: Reactionism, consequences, and care.* Washington, DC: National Academy Press.

Parkes, C. M. (1983). *Recovery from bereavement.* New York: Basic Books.

Peterson, L. (1997). *Surviving the heartbreak of choosing death for your pet: Your personal guide for dealing with pet euthanasia*. Tempe, AZ: Greentree Publishing.

Quackenbush, J. (1984). Social work in a veterinary hospital: Response to owner grief reactions. In W. J. Kay, A. Nieburg, A. H. Hutscher, R. M. Grey, & E. Carole (Eds.), *Pet loss and human bereavement*. Ames, IA: Iowa State University Press.

Quackenbush, J. (1985). The death of a pet: How it can affect pet owners. *Veterinary Clinics of North America: Small Animal Practice, 15*, 305-402.

Quackenbush, J., & Graveline, D. (1985). *When your pet dies: How to cope with your feelings*. New York: Simon & Schuster.

Quackenbush, J., & Voith, V. (Eds.) (1985, March). The veterinary clinics of North America. Small animal practice. *Symposium on the human-companion animal bond*. Philadelphia, PA: W. B. Saunders Company.

Rando, T. A. (1984). *Grief, dying, and death: Clinical interventions for caregivers*. Champaign, IL: Research Press Company.

Rando, T.A. (1986). *Loss and anticipatory grief*. Lexington, MA: Lexington Books.

Raphael, B. (1983). *Anatomy of bereavement*. New York: Basic Books.

Ressier, R. (1998, June 23). Animal cruelty may be a warning. *Washington Times*.

Robin, M., & ten Bensel, R. (1984). *Pets and the family*. New York: Haworth Press.

Robin, M., & ten Bensel, R. (1985). Pets and the socialization of children. Special issue: Pets and the family. *Marriage and Family Review, 8*:3-4, 63-78.

Rogers, F. (1988). *Mr. Rogers' first experience: When a pet dies*. New York: G. P. Putnam's Sons.

Ross, C., & Sorenson, J. (1998). *Pet loss and human emotion: Guiding clients through grief*. New York: Accelerated Development.

Roth, D., LeVier, E. (1990). *Being human in the face of death*. Santa Monica, CA: IBS Press.

Savishinsky, J. S. (1988). The value of cat ownership to elderly women living alone. *International Journal of Aging and Human Development, 27*:4, 241-260.

Schneider, R. (1979). *Pet ownership: Some factors and trends*. Proceedings of the Second Canadian Symposium on Pets and Society, 142-144.

Shirley, V., & Mercier, J. (1983). Bereavement of older persons: Death of a pet. *The Gerontologist, 23*, 276.

Sibbitt, S. (1991). *Oh, where has my pet gone? A pet loss memory book*. Wayzata, MN: B. Libby Press.

Sife, W. (1993). *The loss of a pet*. New York: Howell Book House.

Smart, D., Welch, D., & Zawistoski, R. (1991). *Encountering death: Structured activities for death awareness*. New York: Accelerated Development.

Smith, K. (Ed.) (1997). *Healing the pain of pet loss: Letters in memoriam*. Philadelphia, PA: Charles Press.

Smith, P. (1997). *Animal death, A spiritual journey*. Cumberland, RI: Pegasus Publications.

Smith, P. (1966). *Animals: Our return to wholeness*. Cumberland, RI: Pegasus Publications.

Spiegelman, V., & Kastenbaum, R. (1900). Pet Rest Cemetery: Is eternity running out of time? *Omega, 21*, 1-13.

Steinbach, D. (1997). *Loving, caring, letting go without guilt: A compassionate but straightforward look at pet euthanasia*. Bowie, MD: Willow Bend Publishing.

Stern, M., & Cropper, S. (1998). *Loving and losing a pet: A psychologist and a veterinarian share their wisdom*. St. Northvale, NJ: Jason Aronson.

Stewart, M. (1983). Loss of a pet—Loss of a person: A comparative study of bereavement. In A. H. Katcher & A. M. Beck (Eds.), *New perspectives on our lives with companion animals* (pp. 390-407). Philadelphia, PA: University of Pennsylvania Press.

Stimuli, V. L., & Pratt, C. (1986). Special friends: Elders and pets. *Generations, 10*:4, 44-45.

Stockton, A. (1999). *Honeybun*. Seattle, WA: Educare Press.

Straub, S. H. (2001). *Death without notice*. Amityville, NY: Baywood Publishing Company, Inc.

Straub, S. H. (2002). *Death 101: A workbook for educating and healing*. Amityville, NY: Baywood Publishing Company, Inc.

Stroebe, W., & Stroebe, M. (1987). *Bereavement and health: The psychological and physical consequences of partner loss*. New York: Cambridge University Press.

Sussman, M. (Ed.) (1985). *Pets and the family*. Bridgehampton, NY: Haworth Press, Inc.

Tousley, M., & Heuerman, K. (1997). *The final farewell: Preparing for and mourning the loss of your pet*. Phoenix, AZ: Our Pals Publishing.

Veevers, J. (1992). *What is a pet? Defining the Concept of Companion Animal*. Abstracts and Proceedings, The 6th International Conference on Human-Animal Interactions, Animals and Us, Montreal, Quebec, Presentation #409 ABV, July 22.

Ven Katraman, S. (1992). *Animals and tribals: A case of different harmony*. Abstracts and Proceedings, The 6th International Conference on Human-Animal Interactions, Animals and Us, Montreal, Quebec, July 21-25.

Viorst, J. (1971). *The tenth good thing about Barney*. New York: Aladdin Books, Macmillan Publishing Company.

Wagner, T. L. (1998). *Legacies of love: A gentle guide to healing from the loss of your animal loved one* (audiotape). Matter of the Heart.

Weisman, A. D. (1991). Bereavement and companion animals. *Omega, 22*, 241-248.

White, E. B. (1952). *Charlotte's web*. New York: Dell Publishing Company.

Wilbur, R. H. (1976). *Pets, pet ownership and animal control: Social and psychological attitudes*. Proceedings of the National Conference on Dog and Cat Control, American Humane Association, Denver, Colorado.

Wilhelm, H. (1985). *I'll always love you*. New York: Crown Publishers, Inc.

Wolfelt, A. (1983). *Helping children cope with grief*. Indiana: Accelerated Development, Inc.

Worden, J. W. (1982). *Grief counseling and grief therapy: A handbook for the mental health practitioner*. New York: Springer Publishing Company.

Yoxall, A., & Yoxall, D. (1979). Proceedings of Meeting of Group for the Study of Human Companion Animal Bond, Dundee, Scotland.

Epilogue

BOGEY

On February 25th, as I was leaving the golf course where I worked part-time, one of the guys in the cart barn came up to me with this teeny, tiny kitten sitting in his hand! I couldn't believe how small it was and how sad looking. Of course, when I came back to reality, I said "Oh no, I can't go home with this kitten! My husband will kill me!" It's not that Paul doesn't like animals; he loves all animals, but it is so difficult to deal with their death once you get attached to them. And, it seems like every stray in the world finds me! I knew the golf course was having trouble with stray cats in the cart barn and they had contacted Animal Control to catch the female and several older kittens that were running around and having babies. It also was a dangerous place for them to be—several had already been run over by golf carts and so it was time to clear them out. All were taken away—so they thought! Well, needless to say, I came home with Bogey that afternoon after stopping at my veterinarian's office to make sure he was healthy. I was told my baby kitten was only three weeks old and would have to be fed with an eyedropper until he learned to eat on his own. His eyes had only been open for a couple of days. Not only did he have to be fed with an eyedropper, but I also had to massage his butt to help him relieve himself. Mother cats will lick their young in the genital area until they urinate and/or have a bowel movement. Well, I was not going that far so I massaged Bogey's butt every time I fed him—several times a day! I couldn't wait to get home to take care of him! It was like having a baby in the house. He was so adorable—as cute as a button—and not much bigger than one! :>)

152 / PET DEATH

Bogey

All was well after Paul accepted Bogey. It only took a couple of days before Bogey won him over! You couldn't help but love him! He wanted to play rough and so rough he got! Paul would toss him around and he would come back strong for more. He would play so hard and fast that we were amazed how much he took as a cat. He played like a dog. I used to call him a "Cog" (half cat and half dog!). As he got older we noticed he would stop to rest for a few moments. He would get so tired, but if you stopped playing with him, he would attack your hand forcing you to keep playing. He was so funny! And, we thought it was cute the way his tongue would hang out the side of his mouth. Little did we know our little Bogey Boy had a heart condition! After having lunch with a friend, I came home and found Bogey dead on the bathroom floor! He was only eight months old! It was horrible! I couldn't believe what had happened! My baby was dead! I called Paul and he came home from work. We went straight to our veterinarian and they took Bogey from us and prepared for his cremation. Paul and I were totally devastated. We couldn't understand. How could this happen to our baby cat?! He had his whole life ahead of him.

As a grief counselor and death educator, most people might think it would be easy for me to get through Bogey's death since I am always helping others do just that. However, this isn't any easier for me than it is for my readers. I put off writing this story for over a month before I could actually sit down here and do this. Not only did I write the book, I am now living the words within it.

Just after starting *Pet Death*, our cat Oscar disappears as I mentioned earlier in the book. It is very unusual for us to have a pet disappear—or even die young. Mama was 21 when we had her euthanized. Misty was 14. Barney was 14. Only B.J. died at one year of age after being hit by a car. Ironically, Oscar's disappearance began the book and Bogey's death is ending it. It has been almost two months since Bogey died and it still hurts so much. It will, I'm sure, for a long time. How appropriate it is to add Bogey to the end of this book as a memorial to a cat well loved and adored.

—Sandi Straub

Index

Abuse, animal
  annoying pet habits, preventing, 89–91
  At Twice the Price, 94–95
  caring properly for animals and preventing, 88–89
  child, when abuse appears to be caused by a, 86–87
  Dog's Plea, A, 96
  education, preventive, 87–88, 92–94
  evaluate the situation, 85–86
  examples, serious, 91–92
  Humane Society, contacting the, 85
  laws, learn about local/state, 87
  overpopulation of animals, preventing the, 92–94
  Problem of Pain, The, 95–96
  reporting incidents, 86
  violent pathology in humans, first sign of a, 83–85
Accept the feelings that come with grief
  Kübler-Ross's theories on grief, 50
  [Accept the feelings that come with grief]
  right to feel anger/pain/guilt, 55–56
  Worden's theories on grief, 51
Accident, The (Carrick), 14
Accidents. *See* Suddenly, when a pet dies
Anaxandrides, 109
Anderson, John, 38–42
Anger list, 99
Anger stage in Kübler-Ross's theories on grief, 50
Animal Death, A Spiritual Journey (Smith), 74
Animal Defense League Fund (ADLF), 91
Animals, Our Return to Wholeness (Smith), 74
Animal shelters and coping with the loss of your pet, 57
Annoying pet habits, stopping animal abuse by preventing, 89–91

Antifreeze out of reach of animals, keeping, 89
Apologize for being upset, feeling the need to, 44
Aquinas, Saint Thomas, 73
Aristotle, 73
Attachment theory, 49–50
Attig's (Thomas) theories on grief, 52
At Twice the Price, 94–95

Bargaining stage in Kübler-Ross's theories on grief, 50
Blake, William, 5
Boatswain (Byron), 71–72
Body, dealing with the dead, 10, 69–71
Bond between human and pet, 5–7, 44, 52, 98
Bowers, Clint, 91
Bowlby's (John) theories on grief, 49–50
Brehm, Derek, 91
Bridge Called Love, A, 75
Buddhism, 73
Burials, pet, 69–70
Butler, Samuel, 63

Captain of the Lady Anne, The (McGregor), 6–7
Carbon Canyon Christian School, 91
Carrick, Carol, 14
Cars, pets chasing, 90
Cars and animal abuse, 88–89
Cary, Joyce, 53
Celebration of life scrapbook, 99–100
Cemeteries, pet, 69–71

Children
abuse, animal, 86–87
euthanized pets, 19
explaining/talking with children about death experience, 33–36
Great Truths About Life That Little Children Have Learned, 110
journal writing, 101–103
Christianity, 73
Christmas at Rainbow Bridge, 140–141
Cocoanut Grove Fire in Boston (1944), 48
Cole, Carroll E., 84
Coleridge, Samuel T., 37
Collage, creating a, 100
Collar size and animal neglect, 88
Columbine High School, 84
Comer, Jim/Ginny, 24–26
Communication and coping with the loss of your pet, 54
Communicators, animal, 74
Community's compassion, 11–12
Companion, loss of an animal
Amadeus, 38–42
elderly people, 37–38
interpersonal relationships affected, 41
police dogs, 39–41
Tribute to a Best Friend, 42
Compassion shown to animals, 115–117
Complicated grief, 45–46
Consistency and coping with the loss of your pet, 54
Continuing Bonds (Klass, Silverman & Nickman), 52
Coping with the loss of your pet
communication, 54
consistency, 54

[Coping with the loss of your pet]
  counseling, 56–57
  education, 55
  exercise, 54
  feelings, 55–56
  I'm Still Here, 57–58
  journalizing, 57
  memorials, 55
  nutrition, 53
  sleep, 53
  Tribute to Our Best Friend, A, 58
  See also Healing activities
Counseling, 56–57, 60–61, 98
Creation, The, 61
Cremation, 70

Dahmer, Jeffrey, 84
Darwin, Charles, 3
Dead Cat Test, 114
Deluga, Marty, 109–110
Denial stage in Kübler-Ross's theories on grief, 50
Depression stage in Kübler-Ross's theories on grief, 50
DeSalvo, Albert, 84
Descartes, Rene, 73
Dickinson, Emily, 73
Disabled pets, 113–114
Disappears, when a pet suddenly, 10
Disenfranchised grief, 45, 51, 55–56, 97
Dog Named Spike, A (Olechowski), 23–24
Dogs in Heaven?, 76–77
Dog's Plea, A, 96
Domestic abuse linked to animal abuse, 84
Donations to animal-related causes, 11, 70

Doors, when your pet tries to escape through open, 90
Doris Day Animal Foundation, 93, 94

Eastern views on spirituality, 73
Education
  abuse/neglect prevention through, 87–88, 92–94
  coping with the loss of your pet, 55
Elderly pet owners, 5–6, 37–38
Emotional expression and Worden's (William) theories on grief, 51
Employers' supporting bereaved pet owners, 60
Epilogue (Bogey), 151–153
Eulogy, writing a, 99
Euphemisms, 3, 35–36
Euthanized, when a pet is
  Alex, 24–26
  Bambi, 22
  Buster, 27–30
  Daisy, 26
  Dog Named Spike, A, 23–24
  financial aspects, 18, 19
  goodbye to your pet, saying, 20
  healing activities, 104–105, 107
  His Apologies, 26–27
  home, having procedure done in your, 21
  Last Battle, The, 30–31
  Mickey, 24
  new pet, getting a, 79, 104–105
  procedure is performed, understanding how, 19–20
  Shellie, 21–22
  telling other family members, 19

[Euthanized, when a pet is]
  vets who do their own pets,
    66–67
  when is right time to have
    procedure done, 17–18
  witnessing the procedure,
    20–21
Exercise and coping with the loss
  of your pet, 54

Family loss and getting a new,
  79–80
Feelings and coping with the loss
  of your pet, 55–56
Food allergies, 114–115
Francis of Assisi, Saint, 73
Freud's (Sigmund) theories on
  grief, 47–48

Genogram, pet, 101
Glossary, 121–125
*Great Truths About Life That
  Little Children Have
  Learned*, 110
Grief process, the
  apologize for being upset,
    feeling the need to, 44
  Attig's theories, 52
  Bowlby's theories, 49–50
  complicated grief, 45–46
  Freud's theories, 47–48
  intense grief over loss of pet is
    normal, 42–44, 55–56
  Kübler-Ross outlines five
    stages of grief, 50
  Lindermann's theories, 48–49
  overlooked area (pet loss) in
    grief assessment, 43
  Parkes' theories, 50
  pets grieve, do, 65–67, 109–110
  Rando's theories, 51

[Grief process, the]
  theories on, 46–47
  Worden's theories, 50–51
Grief work, 47, 48–49
Grooming and animal neglect,
  88
Groover, Richard L., 92
Guilt, dealing with, 63–64

Hammarskjold, Dag, 97
Happy endings
  Coco, 114–115
  compassion shown to animals,
    115–117
  Dead Cat Test, 114
  disabled pets, 113–114
  God, dog letters to, 117–119
  grief experienced by pets,
    109–110
  How to Bathe the Cat, 119
  intelligent pets, 117
  Papa, a miracle story about,
    110–113
Harris, Eric, 84
Healing activities
  anger list, 99
  celebration of life scrapbook,
    99–100
  children, pet journal for,
    101–103
  collage, create a, 100
  eulogy, write a, 99
  genogram, pet, 101
  journal writing, 98–99,
    101–103
  Maggie, 103–105
  Scootie, 105–107
  suppress feelings, don't, 97
  See also Coping with the loss of
    your pet
Heaven, pets going to, 74
Heels, when your dog nips at, 90

Helping the bereaved pet owner, 59–62, 127–136
Hinduism, 73
His Apologies (Kipling), 26–27
Holloman, Jackie, 105–107
Holmes, Oliver W., 57
Hospices and coping with the loss of your pet, 57
How to Bathe the Cat, 119
Hughes, Margie A., 136
Humane Society, 85

If Dogs Were Our Teachers, 125–126
I'm Still Here, 57–58
In Memoriam . . . for my cat, Buddy, 1991-2002 (Jones), 81
International Association of Pet Cemeteries (IAPC), 70
Interpersonal relationships affected by loss of animal, 41

Jainism, 73
Jones, Helen A., 81
Journals/newsletters/magazines, 137–138
Journal writing, 57, 98–99, 101–103

Karcher, Harry A., 22
Kiebold, Dylan, 84
Kinkel, Kip, 84
Kipling, Rudyard, 1–2, 26–27
Koplewicz, Harold S., 84
Kübler-Ross (Elisabeth) outlines five stages of grief, 50

Last Battle, The, 30–31
Lewis, C. S., 95–96

Life pattern adjustments and Worden's theories on grief, 51
Lindermann's (Erich) theories on grief, 48–49
Little Dog Angel, A, 75–76
Lost pets, 10–11

Magazines/journals/newsletters, 137–138
Mange and animal neglect, 88
McCabe, Jim, 26
McGregor, Patricia, 6–7
McNiel, Andy, viii
Mead, Margaret, 84
Memorabilia, pet, 139–140
Memorials/ceremonies in memory of the pet, 11–12, 33, 42, 55, 71–72, 153
Miller, Colleen, 61–62
Mourning
  Lindermann's theories on grief, 48
  Rando's theories on grief, 51
  Worden's theories on grief, 50–51
Mummification, 70–71
My Cat, 80

National Pet Memorial Day, 75
Neglect, animal, 88
  See also Abuse, animal
Neuter clinics, 93–94
New pet, getting a, 66, 79–81, 104–105
Newsletters/magazines/journals, 137–138
Nursing homes, companion-animal visits to, 37

Nutrition and coping with the loss of your pet, 53

Olechowski, Robert, 23–24
Organizations, support, 127–136
Outdoors, animal abuse/neglect and leaving animals, 89
Overpopulation of animals, preventing the, 92–94

Parkes' (Colin M.) theories on grief, 50
Patience with oneself and others experiencing loss, 45
People for the Ethical Treatment of Animals (PETA), 91
Phantom (Hughes), 136
Plants, when pets eat your, 89
Poem for Cats, 76
Police dogs, 39–41
Power of the Dog, The (Kipling), 1–2
Problem of Pain, The (Lewis), 95–96

Radner, Gilda, xi
Rainbow Bridge, ix
Rando's (Therese) theories on grief, 51
Rasmussen, Jane, 24
Relearning the world and Attig's theories on grief, 52
Resolution of the grief process and Lindermann's theories on grief, 48
Resources, support, 127–138
Ressier, Robert K., 83

Rhoden, Donna M., 27–30
Rin-Tin-Tin, 70
Robinson, William, 91

Sahib-John, Taramati, 14–15
Sarnoff, David, 59
Scamorza, JoAnn, 21–22
Schweitzer, Albert, 83, 95
Scott, Walter, 65
Sherrill, Patrick, 83
Shock/disbelief and Lindermann's theories on grief, 48
Shriner, Earl K., 83
Sleep and coping with the loss of your pet, 53
Smith, Penelope, 74
Souls, animal, 73–74
Spay clinics, 93–94
Spencer, Brenda, 83
Spirituality, pets and
  Bridge Called Love, A, 75
  communicators, animal, 74
  Dogs in Heaven?, 76–77
  heaven, pets going to, 74
  Little Dog Angel, A, 75–76
  Poem for Cats, 76
  souls, animal, 73–74
Stolen pets, 10
Straub, Sandi, 151–153
Suddenly, when a pet dies
  Bogey, 152–153
  ceremony/service in memory of the pet, 11–12
  community's compassion, 11–12
  disappearances, 10
  illness/health condition, 10
  lost pets, 10–11
  Otis, 12–13
  traffic accidents, 9, 14–15

Support for bereaved pet owners, 59–62, 127–136
Surviving animals, 65–66

Taxidermy, 70
To Love Again, 80–81
Traffic accidents, 9, 14–15
Trent, Cheryl, 103–105
Tribute to a Best Friend, 42
Tribute to Our Best Friend, A, 58
Twain, Mark, 95

Unresolved grief, 45, 51, 55–56, 97

Venter, Elsabe, 114–115
Volunteering time at pet hospitals/cemeteries/Humane Society, 64

Wesley, John, 73
Western views on spirituality, 73
Whyte, Laura, 110–113
Wood, Rose M., 12–13
Woodham, Luke, 84
Worden's (William) theories on grief, 50–51

For Product Safety Concerns and Information please contact our EU
representative GPSR@taylorandfrancis.com
Taylor & Francis Verlag GmbH, Kaufingerstraße 24, 80331 München, Germany

www.ingramcontent.com/pod-product-compliance
Lightning Source LLC
Chambersburg PA
CBHW070617300426
44113CB00010B/1567